Women Crossing Boundaries

*a psychology of
immigration and
transformations
of sexuality*

Oliva M. Espín

ROUTLEDGE
New York and London

01-670

Published in 1999 by
Routledge
29 West 35th Street
New York, NY 10001

Published in Great Britain by
Routledge
11 New Fetter Lane
London EC4P 4EE

Printed in the United States of America on acid-free paper.
Design and typography: Jack Donner

Library of Congress Cataloging-in-Publication Data

Espín, Oliva M.
Women crossing boundaries : a psychology of immigration
and transformations of sexuality / by Oliva M. Espín.
p.   cm.
Includes bibliographical references.
ISBN 0–415–91699–2. — ISBN 0–415–91700–X (pbk.)
1. Women immigrants.   2. Emigration and immigration—Psychological aspects.
3.   Women immigrants—Sexual behavior.   4. Sex role.
I. Title.
HQ1154.E76   1999
305.48'9691—dc21   98–25914
CIP

10   9   8   7   6   5   4   3   2   1

To Nery, for being the other half of my identity

To Dorys, for making it possible

Contents

Acknowledgments   ix

Introduction   1

1   Women's Experience of Migration   15

2   Collecting Immigrant Women's Life Narratives   37

3   The Stories   55

4   Migration, Sexuality, and the Preservation   123
    of Culture and Tradition

5   Language: Identity, Silence, and Sexuality   133

6   Mothers, Daughters, and Migration   145

7   The Experience of Lesbian Immigrants   153

8   Final Thoughts   161

Appendix A   167

References   171

Index   183

Acknowledgments

This book is dedicated to women who have been important in my life in very different ways.

Nery, my sister, playmate, confidante, and dear friend, has been a constant presence in my life. Our shared childhood and the lived and unlived dreams will never disappear; we always hold each other's dreams in our hearts. In many ways, she is the person I could have been and will never be. Conversely, I have lived many dreams and possibilities closed to her because of the turns in her life. No other person, ever, has been as significant in my life as she has been. For all her warmth and support, for the blessing of her sisterly love, for all the beauty of her soul, I want to thank her.

I had promised Dorys 25 years ago that I would dedicate a book to her as an expression of love and gratitude. Life took many turns since that promise. I have acknowledged her contributions to my life and professional development in previous books, but this is her promised dedication. Her presence and loving support eased my adaptation to life in the United States. Many significant life changes happened through her. I will always be thankful for all her caring and patience with me.

Writing this book has, rather unexpectedly, brought back memories of many other people and places who were integral to my life in Cuba. As we were building memories together, we had no idea that most of our lives would be lived away from those people and places. In the intervening years, I have lost touch with many of them. Perhaps this is befitting, since migrations have this effect; people who leave their homeland easily lose track of each other. Those childhood and youth friends symbolize some parts of my life lost forever as a consequence of migration. Parts of my life that were born then are still very much with me. As such, this book is also dedicated to all those people I have lost as a consequence of migration.

I also want to thank the many people who have contributed to this book's creation. First and foremost, I am grateful to the women interviewed. Although their names and identifying information have been changed to preserve their privacy, they will recognize their own stories despite the distortions demanded by confidentiality. Those stories have breathed life into this book. I appreciated their trust. As I describe their experiences, I am conscious that I have not so much "translated" their stories as co-created them. I am aware that representation is never mere description, and narratives are never an exact equivalent of experience.

Besides the main study that forms this book's basis, parts of two small unpublished studies I conducted several years ago (in collaboration with students) are also included in this book. One of these smaller studies was carried out by Aureet Bar-Yam, a student under my direction at Boston University in the early 1980s. This study focused on the connections and disconnections created by migration during adolescence. Aureet died several years ago trying to save her dog from drowning. This tragic accident cut short a young life full of intellectual promise. Her legacy lives in the pages of this book through the stories of two of the adolescents she interviewed.

A third source of data is the stories from a study of mothers and daughters who had been prematurely separated through the vicissitudes of migration. This study was done collaboratively with three students at Tufts University: Nahid Yazdi Paydarfar, Anne Cavanaugh Sawan, and Ruth Marsach Wood. They helped design the study, interviewed participants, and analyzed data. I thank them for their efficient assistance with that project.

Once again, collegial support at the Department of Women's Studies at San Diego State University has crucially nurtured the development of my work. In particular, Susan E. Cayleff continues to be a dear friend and a skilled editor. Without her help, this book never would have seen the light of day. I deeply appreciate her support and presence in my life.

The main research for this book was conducted during a sabbatical year from San Diego State University. As a visiting scholar at the Northwest Center for Research on Women at the University of Washington in Seattle (Fall 1994) and at the Institute for Research on Women and Gender at Stanford University (Spring 1995), I benefited from the environment of collegueship. Angela Ginorio, Laura Brown, and Sherri Matteo were instrumental in facilitating my sabbatical affiliations during that year.

Post-sabbatical, a small grant from the College of Arts and Letters at San Diego State University supported the transcription of interviews. A Grant-in-Aid from the Society for the Psychological Study of Social Issues (Division 9, American Psychological Association) eased the acquisition of resources and facilitated the collection and analysis of data. A mini-grant from the California School of Professional Psychology provided the opportunity for collaboration with Valory Mitchell and the assistance of students.

In the last three years, I have presented preliminary insights at conferences and seminars. Published papers have also resulted from emerging ideas. Contacts through these venues have pushed me to clarify my thinking and interpretations. In particular I would like to acknowledge the contributions of the following people and professional events to the development of this book: Sue Wilkinson, editor of the journal *Feminism and Psychology*, who invited me to present a paper in London, published it in the journal, and later included it in a collection of feminist psychology articles. She and Celia Kitzinger stimulated the international interest in my study. The trip to London was funded through a fellowship I received from the British Psychological Society. Others also encouraged me with their interest in this topic: Mehmet Necef and Yvonne Mørck of the Universities of Odense and Copenhagen in Denmark invited me to present on women and migration at their respective universities. Gabriel Horenczyk of the Hebrew University in Jerusalem invited me to present at a conference on immigration and the development of identity; that paper was published in the conference proceedings. Esther Rothblum from the University of Vermont asked me to present the data on the lesbian interviewees at the Vermont Primary Prevention Conference on Preventing Heterosexism and Homophobia. She and Lynne Bond published that paper in the book based on conference proceedings. Beverly Greene and Marny Hall published other versions of the data on lesbians in the journals *Psychological Perspectives on Lesbian and Gay Issues* and *Women and Therapy*, respectively. Cheryl Travis, as president of Division 35 (Psychology of Women) of the American Psychological Association, and Corann Okorodudu and the members of the Section on Black Women of the same division invited me to present relevant portions of the study at the association's convention. Finally, I presented a paper at the request of Angelika Kofler and the organizers of the 1996 EuroConference on Collective Identities and Symbolic Representation held in Paris. They have recently published a paper on the role of emotion in women's migration based on that presentation in *Innovations: The European Journal of Social Sciences*.

Students and professionals who have taken courses or workshops with me on the experiences of immigrant and refugee women over the last 25 years have been invaluable. Most recently those in my seminar on Women's Experience of Migration at San Diego State University in 1997 and 1998 have contributed to clarify the book's ideas.

The many therapy clients I worked with during my years as a clinician taught me much about the differences and similarities in their experiences as immigrants. Their journeys helped to inspire and form the questions for my research.

Amy Mahoney and Gabriela Garcia-Quan assisted with library research at the early stages of this project. Stacy Watnick-Buhbe, Claire Jackson, and Teresa Alvarez Romero transcribed the audio-tapes of the interviews. Heather Berberet patiently checked references, prepared tables, and took care of other mechanical details while assisting me with teaching. Inge Hansen typed portions of the manuscript. Joanne Ferraro read and commented on the manuscript.

Veronica Castillo graciously and efficiently helped me reconstruct the manuscript when, at the eleventh hour, I thought it was lost. Both she and Heather Berberet saved me from my incompetence with computers and modern technology.

At Routledge, Philip Rappaport believed in the book's concept. More recently, Heidi Freund, Lai Moy, Sarita Sahni, and Liana Fredley have provided assistance and support in its creation.

Last but not least, I would like to thank other women in my life from whose experiences of migration I have also learned: Lourdes Rodríguez-Nogués, Virginia Aponte, María de los Angeles Domínguez, Raquel Matas, Esther Rothblum, and Alina Matas.

To all of them my heartfelt thanks.

Introduction

In 1961 I left my country of birth, Cuba, and started life as an immigrant in Spain, Panama, and Costa Rica. Later circumstances brought me to Belgium and to Canada at different points in my life. Finally, I came to reside in the United States. Although I have been a citizen of the United States for 20 years, my life has been marked by the experience of migration: I have lived my adult life removed from my country of birth. I possess the vague certainty that I could have been another person were it not for the particular circumstances that migration brought into my life. I do not know and will never know the person I could have been had I not left my birth country. The only me I know is the one that incorporates the consequences of migration. Even though my life has been very rich in experiences, and I have never felt particularly deprived, I know that whatever I have succeeded in creating and living has been developed at the expense of some significant losses. Of these losses I am only vaguely aware. Far more clear are the undeniable opportunities, achievements, successes, and fulfillments brought about by migration. For the person who has migrated, identity issues are further complicated by their polyvalent circumstances. One is aware that both life's losses and failures and life's possibilities and triumphs are magnified and distorted by the lens of the migration experience. Migration for me, as for most immigrants, has provided a dual and contradictory legacy. It has given me safety and success, yet it also has brought losses and silence about them. Mention of them is easily confused with self-pity or even ungratefulness to the new country.

My professional work as a teacher, therapist, and scholarly researcher has been centered on issues brought about by the psychological experience of migration (e.g., Cole, Espín, & Rothblum, 1992; Espín, 1996b; 1997). Yet this book focuses more specifically on some of those issues than my previous books have. Here I explore how questions of cultural and sexual identity are developed and negotiated by immigrant and refugee women.

This book is based on two study questions. The first is the broader and more encompassing. It asks what, if any, are the transformations of gender roles and sexuality experienced by women as a consequence of migration? This question is presented against the backdrop of the larger context in which these personal transformations are occurring. The second question is more specific and yet less precise. It explores the relationship of language—specifically, the ability to speak more than one—to the sexual life of the immigrant. It asks whether there is a connection between the language spoken and the experience of one's sexuality and gender roles. Throughout the book, I examine the part that mothers and older women play as role models and transmitters of cultural views on sexuality and gender roles to younger women and girls.

Women's experience of migration is a frequently neglected aspect of migration studies (Espín, 1995, 1997; Hondagneu-Sotelo, 1992, 1994; Pedraza, 1991). I focus on issues of gender roles and sexuality because they are central to the experience of migration as it is lived by women. My focus on language emerged organically, first from my experience as a practicing therapist working with bilingual women and eventually from research: Almost all the women I interviewed talked about language when discussing issues of sexuality. Finally, the role of mothers and motherhood in women's lives is of undisputed importance.

The Global Context

A large proportion of the world's immigrants and refugees are women. The United Nations estimates that 80 percent of all refugees in the world are women and their children (U.S. Committee for Refugees, 1990; U.N.-INSTRAW, 1994; U.N.-IMPSF, 1995; UNHCR, 1997). Further, at least half the people who migrate internationally for economic reasons are women (U.N.-INSTRAW, 1994; U.N.-IMPSF, 1995). Currently it is estimated that the foreign-born population in the United States is about 20 million (Portes & Rumbaut, 1996; Rogler, 1994). Women account for more than 55% of persons admitted as relatives of U.S. citizens (U.N.-INSTRAW, 1994; U.N.-IMPSF, 1995).

The United Nations unequivocally states in a recent document that:

> Improving the status of women is increasingly recognized as fundamental to improving the basic human rights of over half the population of the world and also contributing to socioeconomic progress. . . . Women's migration, both internally within developing countries and internationally across borders . . . to developed countries, is inextricably linked to the status of women in society. (U.N.-INSTRAW, 1994, p. 1)

This assertion is followed by questions yet unanswered:

> But what do we know about women's migration? . . . For example, does migration lead to improvements in the status of women, breaking down patriarchal structures and enhancing women's autonomy or does it lead to perpetuate dependency? (U.N.-INSTRAW, 1994, p. 1).

Anthropologist Emmanuel Todd (1994) believes that the defining factor in the adjustment of immigrants—the factor that determines the ultimate success of the migration process for a specific group—is the social status of women in both the country of birth and the country of reception. He sees the freedom—or lack of it—afforded women in both contexts as the most important anthropological indicator of the quality of the experience of migration for any group. According to him, this is the crucial factor in the immediate "destiny of immigrants." Todd bases his position on historical and anthropological data on migration in France, Germany, England, and the United States. One of Todd's most significant arguments is that exogamy—intermarriage between immigrants and members of the host society—is an indicator of integration and a marker of successful migration. This is a condition, one might add, that becomes further complicated for immigrants from "racialized" groups.

Although I do not fully agree with all of Todd's perspectives, I do concur with his idea that the degree of integration of the women of a given immigrant group in the host society—rather than the integration and/or success of men—indicates the significance of the transformations occurring in the immigrant community. It signals their adaptation to the new life.

It is my contention that migration—and the acculturation process that follows—opens up different possibilities for women than for men. Migration impacts gender roles and sexual behavior in profoundly different ways for women (e.g., Espín, 1984, 1987b, 1995, 1996a, 1996b; Espín et al., 1990; Goodenow & Espín, 1993; Hondagneu-Sotelo, 1994; Pedraza, 1991; Todd, 1994). Frequently, newly encountered sex-role patterns in the "host culture" (i.e., the prevalent culture in the country of reception), combined with greater access to paid employment, create for women the possibility to live a new way of life. Some women become employed outside the home for the first time after the migration. Many of them encounter new opportunities for education. All of them are confronted with the alternative meanings of womanhood provided by observing the lives of women in the host country.

The Impact of Migration on Gender Roles and Sexuality

For both heterosexual and lesbian women, the crossing of borders through migration provides the space and "permission" to cross boundaries and transform their sexuality and sex roles. This happens even in the face of "limited spatial mobility and the culture of virginity" (Necef, 1994, p. 143) that prevail in many immigrant communities.

Women who migrate from "traditional" societies find new alternatives open to them in the new country. They are presented with opportunities afforded to women in the modern world. But the new possibilities that migration opens up are not limited to women who emigrate from traditional societies. Women who migrate from "modern" societies may also find that alternatives open up for them in the new country because of the distance from the familiar environment and, in some cases, from their families. In the realms of sexuality and gender roles as in other areas of life, "new learning opportunities emerge, as host society institutional structures interact with the psychological equipment immigrants bring and create in the host society" (Rogler, 1994, p. 706).

This is usually not a smooth process, even for those women who seem to have acculturated easily to the new society. The internalization of cultural and familial norms has deep roots in the psychology and identity of all human beings. Those who are uprooted from one society, no matter how successfully they adapt to life in another, do not fully let go of the internalized injunctions (Espín, 1992). For women, this is particularly true for those injunctions that affect sexuality and gender-role expectations.

Immigration, even when willingly chosen and eagerly sought, produces a variety of experiences with significant emotional consequences for the individual. I believe with Rogler (1994) that "the psychological study of migrations . . . is first and foremost the study of how social networks are dissembled and reassembled during the cross-cultural movement toward incorporation in the host society" (p. 704). Many women immigrants have had little control over the decision to migrate. This may be due to political circumstances that have precipitated the migration (e.g., Cole, Espín, & Rothblum, 1992) or to patriarchal family structures that afford them little or no decision-making power.

Often women's networks of female friends and extended family are truncated when leaving their birth countries. This predicament necessitates a resourceful reconstruction of the self that may lead to new identity alternatives (e.g., Espín, 1994b). Conversely, the "dissembling of old networks" may encourage the immigrant to resort to rigid behaviors along traditional cultural lines as a defense mechanism against massive loss. This option may be prompted by individual defensive needs, or it can be an imposition from her family or other members of her "home culture" (i.e., the prevalent culture in the country of birth).

Within immigrant communities, traditional gender-role behaviors are often demanded from women migrants. We know that the sexual and gender-role behaviors of women serve a larger social function beyond the personal. They are used by enemies and friends alike as proof of the morality—or decay—of social groups or nations. In most societies, women's sexual behavior and their conformity to traditional gender roles signify the family's value system. Thus in many societies, a daughter who does not conform to traditional morality can be seen as proof of the lax morals of a family. This is why struggles surrounding acculturation in immigrant and refugee families center frequently on issues of daughters' sexual behaviors and women's sex roles in general. For parents and young women alike, acculturation and sexuality are closely connected. In many immigrant communities, to be "Americanized" is seen as almost synonymous with being sexually promiscuous (Espín, 1984, 1987b, 1995).

Moreover, the self-appointed "guardians of morality and tradition" that are ever-present among immigrant communities are deeply concerned with women's roles and sexual behavior (Yuval-Davis, 1992). These guardians include religious or community leaders, older women and men, and even younger people who feel a need to preserve old values at all costs. Since immigrant communities are often besieged with rejection, racism, and scorn, those self-appointed guardians have always found fertile ground from which to control women's sexuality in the name of preserving tradition.

Groups that are transforming their way of life through a vast and deep process of acculturation focus on preserving tradition almost exclusively through the gender roles of women. Women's roles become the "bastion" of tradition, and women's bodies become the site for struggles concerning disorienting cultural differences. Gender becomes the site to claim the power denied to immigrants by racism. The control of women becomes the means of asserting moral superiority in a racist society. As a consequence, women of all ages in immigrant families face restrictions on their behavior. While men are allowed and encouraged to develop new identities in the new country, girls and women are expected to continue living as if they were still in the old country (e.g., with regard to gender-role norms and behavior, clothing, rituals, and so on). They are often forced to embody cultural continuity amid cultural dislocation (Yuval-Davis, 1992).

Some of the rigidity about the roles of women that we observe in immigrant communities is an attempt to protect and safeguard what remains of emotional stability; so much of it is lost with migration. It is as if the immigrants' psychological sense of safety and their sense of self depended on a sharp contrast between two sets of cultural values conceived as rigidly different and unchangeable. The preservation of old versions of women's roles becomes central to this sharp contrast. For people who experience a deep lack of control over their daily lives, controlling women's sexuality and behavior becomes a symbolic demonstration of orderliness and continuity and gives them the feeling that not all traditions are lost. This is why women themselves frequently join in adhering to traditions that, from the point of view of outsiders, appear to curtail their own freedoms and opportunities for self-fulfillment.

It obviously is easier for immigrants to maintain control over their private world than over their public lives—work schedules, types of work and schooling, housing, and the structures of daily life are controlled by the customs and demands of the new society. But in the privacy of their homes, they can seek to maintain the sense that they are still in control. This may be particularly important for males who have lost their sense of importance and authority as a consequence of the migration.

Pressures on immigrant women's sexuality also emerge from outside their own culture. The host society imposes its own burdens and desires through prejudices and racism. While "returning women to their 'traditional roles' continues to be defined as central to preserving national identity and cultural pride" (Narayan, 1997, p. 20) by some immigrants, those same values and behaviors are perceived by their hosts as a demonstration of immigrants' backwardness and need for change. Even in situations where racism may be expressed subtly, the immigrant woman finds herself between what Philomena Essed has termed "gendered racism" (1991, 1994) in the dominant society and the sexist expectations of her own community.

Paraphrasing Nigerian poet and professor 'Molara Ogundipe-Leslie (1993) we could say that immigrant women have several "mountains" on their back, the two most obvious ones being "the heritage of tradition" and "the oppression from outside." The prejudices and racism of the dominant society make the retrenchment into tradition appear justifiable. Conversely, the rigidities of tradition appear to justify the racist or prejudicial treatment of the dominant society. These "two mountains" reinforce and encourage each other. Moreover, the effects of racism and sexism are not only felt as pressure from the outside; like all forms of oppression, they become internalized. Frequently, the internalization of oppression is expressed by women (immigrant or not) through conflicts in the expression of their sexuality (e.g., Bonierbale et al., 1981; Valverde, 1985).

Yet a third oppressive factor comes from people eager to be culturally "sensitive." Under the guise of respect, they may racialize and exoticize immigrant women, particularly those who come from non-European countries. Many well-intentioned people believe that the "true" immigrant has to be "different" even if she does not want to be. Tragically, they contribute to the oppression of immigrant women in the name of respecting their culture and preserving their values. More than once, for example, I have encountered people who justified and accepted the existence of spousal abuse among immigrants as part of their culture—as if family violence did not exist in mainstream American culture. The reality is, as stated very forcefully by Chinese American psychologist Christine Ho (1990)—who has done research on violence in Asian immigrant communities—that "violence against women is oppressive and intolerable, regardless of a woman's cultural and social background" (p. 130). After all, "violence hurts victims physically regardless of cultural heritage and customs" (p. 147). Thus immigrant men "should not be allowed to use their cultural background as an excuse for their abusive behavior" (p. 146). And, we may add, neither should their presumed advocates. In this and other instances, deployment of tradition and culture to justify behavior should never remain unproblematized.

For daughters of immigrant families, the development of their identity as young women becomes intertwined with the acculturation process and the emotional demands of migration. As I posited in my earlier writing:

> If sex roles are problematic for adolescent females in general, this is doubly true for immigrant females, particularly those from more traditional cultures. The immigrant adolescent [girl] is faced with having to adjust to two sex cultures. (Goodenow & Espín, 1993, pp. 176–177)

Emotional resources are strained by the need to cope with two demanding life tasks of primary importance for adolescents: psychological independence from parents and the formation of identity during adaptation to the new society.

The development of identity and adaptation to a new life is further problematized for women and girls who come from non-European backgrounds. These women are confronted with the realities of racial politics in the United States. Because they are racialized individuals immersed in racial politics, their adaptation to the host society is additionally burdensome for them. Racialized immigrant women are assumed to be members of ethnic and racial minorities, which poses additional conflicts and dilemmas. As historian Donna Gabaccia argued, foreign-born women immigrants in the United States resemble each other more regardless of race and ethnicity, "than the native born minorities that they seem to resemble 'racially.'" (1994, p. xvii).

Immigrant women and girls develop their identity against the backdrop of these contradictions. As expressed by Bhavnani and Haraway (1994) in an interview for a special issue of the journal *Feminism & Psychology* on racisms and identities, "these young women in their embodiment, are the points of collision of all these powerful forces, including forces of their own" (p. 33). Sometimes, these contradictions express themselves through emotional or other problems. More often than not, though, most immigrant women and girls appear to remain unscarred and manage to survive and emerge from the emotional struggle created by these contradictions.

I believe we need to reconceptualize how we view women immigrants by expanding our understanding of what migration entails for women. Despite prevalent misconceptions, women immigrants and refugees are "not only victims of structural forces or robots computing cost benefits of their moves" (Hondagneu-Sotelo, 1994, p. 6). Rather they are human agents discovering and creating themselves anew through their "nomadic" experiences (Braidotti, 1994). This book and the studies on which it is based hope to contribute to that perspective, by using the medium of personal narrative to understand the psychology of migration from women's perspective.

For several years I have studied gender-related issues among immigrant and refugee women. I have focused on the main issues and consequences entailed in crossing both geographical and psychological borders and boundaries. More recently, I have turned my attention almost exclusively to issues of sexuality. My interest was motivated by the dearth of material on this subject despite its importance in the lives of women immigrants. Specifically, I have analyzed how sexuality and gendered behavior in women are affected by migration. I have collected life narratives from women who have migrated to the United States over the last half century from different parts of the world—including Austria, Brazil, Canada, China, Cuba, Germany, Haiti, Holland, India, Iran, Ireland, Israel, Jamaica, Japan, Korea, Mexico, Nicaragua, Norway, Perú, Puerto Rico, Russia, Sri Lanka, Tibet, and Turkey.

The data reported in this book are derived from information gathered in three different studies. Whenever I refer to the "main" study without specifying further, I refer to my most recent study, which constitutes the core of the book. The in-depth interviews in this study focused on respondents' individual life stories with particular emphasis on the development and transformation of their sexuality and gender roles. Most of the ideas presented and argued in this book are based on the data derived from this particular study.

The 35 women interviewed for this main study ranged in age from early 20s to mid-70s and were all college educated. They were interviewed in Boston, Chicago, Miami, New York, San Diego, San Francisco, and Seattle over a period of 4 years. The women interviewed were chosen for their ability to articulate their experiences about the research topic and their fluency in English. Knowledge of their first language was expected even though not all of them had the same level of fluency in it. English was the mother tongue of a few of the interviewees (e.g., those who migrated from the British Caribbean). In these cases, accent and regional terminology played the same psychological role that a first language played for the bilingual interviewees.

The results of this study have been enlarged by adding the life narratives of women immigrants from two additional studies. These were carried out under my direction in previous years (Bar-Yam, 1983; Espín et al., 1990). The purpose of the first of these two additional studies (Bar-Yam, 1983) "was to enter a preliminary exploration of the impact of immigration on adolescent development" (p. 1). The study was conducted through an "open-ended, relatively unstructured interview format . . . with a small sample of adolescents" (p. 4). All participants in the study were high school students in their senior year. They had immigrated into the United

States at least 2 years before the interview and all were fluent in English. Two stories from that study were selected for inclusion in this book because they demonstrate some of the core issues under discussion. These two young women, Novena and Iris, were 17 years old at the time of the interview and had come from Russia and Israel, respectively. These two stories expand the perspectives discussed herein. The other narratives from the 1983 study were less relevant than Novena's and Iris's for the purpose of this book and are not included here.

The focus of the second additional study was

> the experience of women who have separated from their mothers during their adolescence and early adulthood due to migration. The purpose of the study was to describe the experience of [these] women . . . to assess the impact of this separation in the life experience of the daughters. (Espín et al., 1990, p. 2)

Some of the participants in this study of mother-daughter relationships and migration had come to the United States as students with no intention of permanently moving away from their birth country. Although their experiences provided data relevant to the 1990 research project, only the experiences of women who were true immigrants to the United States have been included in this book. The participants in the second additional study who have been selected for inclusion in this book—Roya, Mina, Nora, Violeta and Colleen—range in age from mid-20s to early 60s and originate from Iran, Cuba, and Ireland. At the conclusion of the mother-daughter study, another woman, Annette, born in Germany, volunteered to be interviewed. Her story is also included.

These two studies will add to our understanding of women's migration, first, by incorporating the experience of immigrant adolescents described as it is happening rather than in retrospective and second, by expanding the exploration of the impact of migration on women by adding a perspective on the effect of this experience on the mother-daughter relationship. Whenever data or insights from these two additional studies are incorporated in the discussion, this will be made clear.

The stories of these 43 women reveal migration to be an event that disrupts and determines the life course. I perceive their personal narratives as the stories they have created to recover the thread of their own lives after migration. I explore how questions of cultural and sexual identity are developed and negotiated by immigrant and refugee women.

The migration narratives of the interviewees are intertwined with their telling about the development of their sexualities, their relationships, and their identity. Although their personal narratives did not focus exclusively on "the experience of migration" or on "sexuality," these are always interwoven themes. Their stories are the product of unique personal and cultural contexts dislocated by the migration. The events surrounding migration and its precipitants are embodied by these women, whose everyday thoughts, feelings, and desires continue to develop amid larger, uncontrollable, sociohistorical events. Thus, the stories are both prototypes and individual tales. Together, these narratives challenge common stereotypes about immigrant women.

Each individual's life uniquely reveals the themes that emerge as shared experiences. Ultimately, the fact that women from different countries of origin, ages, social classes, and life experiences shared so many themes in common attests to the commonalities experienced by women immigrants across generations, life stages, and historical circumstances.

In summary, this book describes and analyzes women's experience of migration to the United States. It posits that familial and individual conflicts in immigrant communities frequently involve struggles over women's sexuality, sexual behavior, and sex roles. Discourse on the preservation of cultural values usually centers on women's sexuality, although this may not be explicitly stated. To understand the development of immigrant women's and girls' lives, I probe their experiences of migration and the formation of their individual identities.

I became interested in this topic of research as a feminist psychologist providing mental health services to immigrant and refugee women, and my perspective has a strong psychological emphasis. Indeed, the book is primarily intended for psychologists and other mental health professionals. However, due to the nature of the topic, I believe it is important to incorporate insights from outside the discipline of psychology. While I profit from these interdisciplinary insights, I remain aware of the perils of venturing into unknown domains—of migrating into the territory of other disciplines! Scholars of immigration who base their work in other disciplines may find my work wanting and my approach limited; my psychology background inevitably structures and limits my understanding of these women from other disciplinary perspectives. However, it also provides unique and seldom-used lenses through which to examine the lives of women immigrants and the narratives they generate.

Women's Experience of Migration

1

The discipline of psychology has paid little attention to the impact of traumatic historical and political events on psychological development. Other social sciences have sought explanations for human behavior in the cultural context. But for psychology, this is almost a novelty. Although the voices of feminist and cultural psychologists have strongly addressed the impact of cultural forces on the individual, psychology has persisted in using intrapsychic individual explanatory models. The omission of social and cultural factors in psychological theory occurs despite the fact that these forces are central to the psychological development of individuals. Their impact is obvious in the traumatic events of the modern world. A few examples of social, political, and historical traumatic events that can create psychological scars are the Nazi Holocaust, the Vietnam War, and exposure to terrorist attacks. These events can produce emotional responses for several generations.

The experience of immigration into another country, either forced or voluntary, is another example of a life transition that can trigger anxieties and create unique psychological consequences for individuals who migrate. Migration also produces psychological effects for the immigrants' descendants beyond the obvious fact that the younger generations are born or grow into adulthood in the new country. The intergenerational transmission of trauma combines with the psychological transformations prompted by the migration to produce these effects and to influence the nature of parenting and other relationships. Posttraumatic stress, mourning and grieving, acculturative stress, and other phenomena are common among immigrant and refugees. These psychological effects are derived from losses and traumatic experiences, but also from the successes the immigrants may achieve through the process of migration.

Migration is the move from one region, country, or place of abode to settle in another. In this book I use the word migration to describe the geographical move of individuals across national borders for the purpose of residing more or less permanently in a country other than the person's country of birth. Historically, immigration is at the core of the United States as a nation. But throughout history, American attitudes toward immigration and migrants have varied dramatically, from encouragement and receptivity to outright rejection and contempt for immigrants (e.g., Easterlin et al., 1982; Pedraza & Rumbaut, 1996; Portes & Rumbaut, 1996). Globally and nationally, immigration policy has been one of the most important political issues in the 1980s and 1990s.

To understand the psychological impact of migration in the lives of immigrants and refugees, attention needs to be placed on the characteristics of both "the context of exit" and "the context of reception." Both are significant determinants of the success of immigrants' adaptation to their new life (Portes & Rumbaut, 1996).

Migration is motivated by diverse factors including a desire for better economic conditions, fear of political or other forms of persecution,[1] family reunification, and other personal reasons. If economic gain is the main force behind the migration, the person migrating is considered an immigrant. If persecution and danger are the motivating force behind the migration, the person is considered a refugee.

Sociologists Alejandro Portes and Ruben Rumbaut in their book *Immigrant America: A Portrait* (1996), explain that

> The distinction hinges on the notion of refugees as involuntary and relatively unprepared migrants "pushed out" by coercive political conditions or by an "exposure to disaster," versus immigrants as voluntary and better prepared movers "pulled in" by perceived opportunities for economic advancement or family reunification. The distinction is actually more elusive than this definition suggests. (p. 168)

The legal distinction between immigrants and refugees is colored by the political persuasion of governments. Their definitions tend to override the realities of the situation as experienced by the person who migrates (Cole, Espín, & Rothblum, 1992; Pedraza & Rumbaut, 1996; Portes & Rumbaut, 1996; Richmond, 1994).

> "Refugee" is not a self-assigned label, but one assigned by the host government. . . . Differential labeling by the U.S. government has marked, for example, the divergent official receptions and subsequent adaptation experiences of South East Asian boat people, on the one hand, and Central American escapees, on the other. (Portes & Rumbaut, 1996, p. 168)

To avoid the confusion of politically based definitions, I conceptualize the differences between immigrants and refugees from a psychological point of view, *not* on the basis of governmental decisions about who is assigned one status or another. Hence, when I use the terms "immigrant" or "refugee" I refer to the migrant's perception of the situation and the degree of trauma experienced, not their assigned legal status.

Usually refugees have experienced more traumatic events than immigrants. "Although both refugees and immigrants must cope with a significant amount of life change, 'refugees' appear to experience more threat, more undesirable change, and less control over the events that define their context of exit" (Portes & Rumbaut, 1996, p. 169). Higher stress and posttraumatic stress symptoms are found among people who define themselves as refugees (Molesky, 1986), such as "Salvadorans and Guatemalans who came to the United States escaping civil war conditions in their respective native countries [although these people are] not recognized as refugees by the U.S. government" (Portes & Rumbaut, 1996, p. 170).

These higher levels of stress have been found particularly among females (e.g., Salgado de Snyder, 1986; Salgado de Snyder et al., 1990). This phenomenon is more present in women because of traumatic experiences in the process of migration, loss of their networks of female relatives and childhood friends through migration, or lack of participation in the decision to migrate (Salgado de Snyder, 1986; Salgado de Snyder et al., 1990).

In this book I use the terms "migrant" and "immigrant" interchangeably to refer to both immigrant and refugee women. At times I specify when the issues in question apply exclusively to either immigrants or refugees.

In the last several decades, increased interest and awareness concerning the plight of immigrants and refugees have developed worldwide. Accordingly, research studies emerged, and publications addressed migration issues. These studies were informed by the different social science disciplines' perspectives (e.g., Mahler, 1995; Pedraza & Rumbaut, 1996; Portes & Rumbaut, 1996; Richmond, 1994; Todd, 1994). Most research on migration focuses on economic, political, and social variables. When mental health and psychological issues are addressed in this literature, the focus is upon the number and characteristics of psychiatric diagnoses, hospital admissions, and so on. This emphasis overshadows understanding the intrapsychic and personal experiences of immigrants as individuals.

The role of women in international migration has begun to draw attention from researchers, policy makers, and service providers; although it continues to be understudied. Several studies exclusively emphasize women's experience during the migration process in

Europe, the United States, Israel, and other parts of the world (e.g., Andizian et al., 1983; Gabaccia, 1992, 1994; Phizacklea, 1983; U.N.-INSTRAW, 1994; U.N.-IMPSF, 1995). These studies, while valuable, mostly focus on women's struggles to adjust to the external trappings of a new society. In a few cases, they address the subjects' coping with the loss of country and social networks. Some address women's increased involvement in public life, such as labor force participation and educational attainment. This research has clearly established that "immigration has a decided impact on the labor force participation of women" (Pedraza, 1991, p. 311). Still, little is known about the experiences of heterosexual and lesbian immigrant women in the private realm, even though we know that different types of male-female power relations in the family develop as a consequence of migration (Pedraza, 1991). These new types of power relations involve sexuality and other aspects of their emotional and affective lives.

Indeed, as sociologist Sylvia Pedraza emphasizes, "we have yet to develop a truly gendered understanding of the causes, processes, and consequences of migration" (1991, p. 304). Thus "research on immigrant women . . . needs to chronicle . . . the private world of immigrant women and their community, and the contribution immigrant women made to [that] private sphere" (Pedraza, 1991, p. 318).

Regardless of the immigrant's or refugee's eagerness to be in a new country, the transitions they confront often result in loneliness from minimal contact with people who shared past experiences. They also struggle with the strain and fatigue derived from adapting and coping with cognitive overload; feelings of rejection from the new society, which affect self-esteem and may lead to alienation; confusion in terms of role expectations, values, and identity; shock resulting from the differences between the two cultures; and a sense of uprootedness and impotence resulting from an inability to function competently in the new culture (Espín, 1997; Garza-Guerrero, 1974; Taft, 1977).

As migrants cross borders, they also cross emotional and behavioral boundaries. Becoming a member of a new society stretches the boundaries of what is possible in several ways. It also curtails what might have been possible in the country of origin. One's life and roles change. With them, identities change as well. The identities expected and permitted in the home culture are frequently no longer expected or permitted in the host society. Boundaries are crossed when new identities and roles are incorporated into life. Most immigrants and refugees crossing geographical borders rarely anticipate the emotional and behavioral boundaries they will confront.

Psychological Stages of the Migratory Process

On the basis of clinical observations, I have postulated three stages in the process of migration (Espín, 1987b): (a) the initial decision concerning relocation, (b) the actual geographical move into another country, and (c) the adaptation to a new society and way of life. At each step, men and women experience the process differently. In other words, gender is central to the lived experience of migration. For instance, at the decision-making stage, women are frequently not consulted about their preference to leave or stay or are not expected to make those decisions independently. Most men, however, participate in the family decision to leave, or they make the decision themselves. During relocation, particularly if escaping dangerous political conditions, women's physical endurance may be questioned or their vulnerability may be exploited. This may impair their being provided the same opportunities to escape as men. It also may add further trauma through rape and other forms of abuse. At the third stage, when acculturation and adaptation occur, women's gender roles may be modified more dramatically than men's. Their struggles to adapt to the new environment may be further complicated by gender-based cultural prescriptions.

Acculturation and adaptation to a new culture also follows several stages (Arredondo-Dowd, 1981). These include: initial joy and relief, disillusionment with the new country, and, finally, acceptance of the good and the bad in the host country. This process entails some form of psychological reorganization as well as material adjustment and emotional adaptation to the situation (Garza-Guerrero, 1974; Grinberg & Grinberg, 1984). Identity is subject to change throughout life. However, social forms of trauma, such as migration, shake its foundations like nothing else.

Understanding the processes of psychological reorganization necessary for adaptation to another culture is essential for understanding what the experience of migration entails at the intrapsychic level. This process, usually termed acculturation, is at the core of the psychological implications of migration. Acculturation is distinguished from assimilation in that the former does not imply the disappearance of all values, customs, and behaviors originating in the home culture. The emphasis on acculturation rather than assimilation contradicts the melting pot ideology of assimilation. To some degree, acculturation is inevitable for all individuals who migrate. Nevertheless, "acculturation is not a simple solution to the traumas of immigration because it itself becomes a traumatic process" (Portes & Rumbaut, 1996, p. 186). Yet it is not necessarily negatively disruptive. Healthy acculturation can emerge into healthy biculturalism (Szapocznik & Kurtines, 1980).

Regardless of one's gender and cultural background, the process of immigration always involves important psychological changes. These changes continue to evolve throughout the immigrant's life and include the development of a new identity (Garza-Guerrero, 1974). Indeed, "cultural relocation tugs at the very roots of identity" (Levy-Warren, 1987, p. 301). However, "[j]ust how it is that culture plays a role in the process of identity formation and how cultural relocation, therefore, shakes identity to its core have still to be clearly delineated" (Levy-Warren, 1987, p. 302).

The process of adaptation and acculturation is not linear. The multiple intrapsychic and behavioral changes required for successful acculturation occur at many levels. Individuals will experience these changes at their own unique paces. The specific circumstances surrounding the migration also impinge on the process of adaptation. Besides the characteristics of the context of exit and the degree of support or rejection provided by the context of reception, other factors act as modifiers of the experience. These include the possibility of returning to the home country for periodic visits; the magnitude of the differences in culture, values, and religion between home and host countries; previous knowledge of the language of the home country; opportunities for upward mobility and maintenance of one's occupational and social class identity; and racial status as a member of the "majority" or "minority" group. Age is of particular importance in this process. It is common wisdom that children learn faster and adapt better than adults to their new surroundings and language. However, adult immigrants may have the advantage of having achieved the intrapsychic capacity for separateness. This may help them be more adept at tolerating distance from loved ones than children and adolescents who presumably do not yet have this capacity, particularly if the latter migrate unaccompanied by immediate family. For children and adolescents, parents' ability to cope with the stress of the migration and continue performing protective roles (versus disintegrating psychologically under it) is usually a determining factor in successful adaptation.

The pace of acculturation is also a significant factor. The adaptation process may be accomplished so quickly that it produces negative results, including a higher incidence of mental illness, drug dependence, and loss of identity (Portes & Rumbaut, 1996). Several decades ago, in an article that became a classic on this topic, Stonequist (1937) addressed the "inner strain and malaise, a feeling of isolation or not quite belonging" (p. 2) that characterize the experience of what he referred to as "the marginal man"—a term he coined. Conversely, acculturation might never be successfully completed if rejection and distance from the host culture are the preferred modes of coping with the new society and way of life. The traditional role expectations for women in a particular culture may foster their isolation from the mainstream culture, thus stalling the acculturation process.

Although some immigrant women choose to adhere to the traditional roles dictated by their culture, most—particularly young women—find these dysfunctional and unsatisfying in the new environment. Culturally based conflicts may develop in families as women try to reconcile the traditional gender roles of their home culture with the demands of participation in the new environment.

This is particularly true for women who encounter greater access to paid employment and educational opportunities. These new economic, social, and emotional options create an imbalance in the traditional power structure of the family (Torres-Matrullo, 1980). Age and gender weigh heavily in familial-role conflicts among immigrants (Szapocznik & Kurtines, 1980). In many cultures, respect for elders and males goes uncontested until those traditions are confronted with the standards and expectations of the new society. These contradictions of old and new expectations produce explicit distress that emanates from the migratory process and conflicting cultural dictums.

Gender Roles and the Acculturation Process

Immigrant women and girls in the United States attempt acculturation into American society amid ever-changing role expectations for women. Some immigrants come from countries whose official governmental policies or cultural beliefs foster the transformation of women's roles. Others migrate from an urban professional environment that reflects the global feminist movement. In other instances, immigrants come from very traditional rural or religious environments where minimal social change has taken place for years or decades before migration. What is appropriate behavior for women in the host culture may be unclear and confusing for the immigrant. Frequently it is more difficult for women than for men to negotiate "acceptable" behavior. The need or desire to adapt to the host culture is easily interpreted as disrespectful of the home culture's values and those people—usually the older generations—who represent them most ardently.

As previously mentioned, immigrants may become entrenched in traditional social and sex-role norms to defend against strong pressures to acculturate. Here, the home culture (i.e., the cultural values predominant in the country of birth) becomes idealized. Its values, characteristics, and customs become symbolic of the stability in personal identity. Retention of these behaviors is a strong defense against identity loss generated by acculturation. The older generation's attempt to preserve old ways increases intergenerational and gender-role conflicts in the family. Further conflicts related to gender norms develop because women may become increasingly employable in the host country while their husbands or fathers experience a loss of status and authority. Clinicians commonly observe that parents are distressed by their children's rapid pace of acculturation. Similarly, husbands frequently resent their wives' seeming new independence that challenges their patriarchal authority. Research shows that the pace of acculturation tends to be slower for females than males in all aspects but one: Females acculturate faster than males when it comes to gender roles (Ginorio, 1979). This may be reflected in the gender patterns that characterize the desire or reluctance to return to the home country when this possibility is present.

As researchers have found,

> While men were eager to return, . . . women tended to post-pone or avoid return because they realized it would entail their retirement from work and the loss of the new-found freedoms. . . . As a result, a struggle developed over . . . return that revolved around the traditional definitions of gender and privileges which the migration itself had challenged and which many men sought to regain by returning home. (Pedraza, 1991, p. 310)

As previously mentioned, for adolescent girls and young adult women the transitions created by immigration present additional tasks. On the one hand, it is easier for them to adjust to the new way of life since their identity is not yet solidified. On the other, adolescent and young adults lose peers and other emotional guideposts that would have informed their identity development in their former cultural context. Parents' disorientation coupled with the adolescents' greater skill to manage the new culture and language increase the children's fear of being lost and not being able to count on parents for protection from perceived threats in the social and physical environment (e.g., Lieblich, 1993). As Erikson said,

the danger of any period of large-scale uprooting and trans-
migration is that exterior crises will, in too many individuals
and generations, upset the hierarchy of developmental crises
and their built-in correctives; and [make them] lose those
roots that must be planted firmly in meaningful life cycles.
(1964, p. 96)

Complementing Erikson's contention, in past coauthored
research, Goodenow and I argued that psychological development,

apart from the influence of ethnicity and immigration,
[includes] gender as a crucial factor. . . . Not only is sexual
maturity a major hallmark of the transition from childhood
to adulthood, but sex roles have a pervasive influence on
every aspect of adult life. (Goodenow & Espín, 1993, p. 176)

Negotiating gender roles in both the home and host cultures
becomes one of the major developmental tasks for immigrant adolescents. Thus, young women or adolescent girls who migrate with their
families confront the question of how to "become American" without
completely losing their own cultural heritage. Girls frequently
respond to these negotiations through adolescent rebellion against
parental culture. They may refuse to speak their first language at
home, reject cultural customs, and react negatively toward parents
and native culture. Since American society at large encourages immigrants to deny their cultural heritages, the adolescent immigrant
finds ample support from adults in positions of authority to challenge
her parents' values. Conflicts over parental authority often are played
out around issues of appropriate sexual behavior: Dating and other
behaviors related to sexuality become the focus of conflict between
parents and daughters[2] (Espín, 1984, 1987b, 1995).

The experiences of women who migrate alone may be different
from those women who migrate in family units. Women who migrate
alone experience some unique struggles. Their loneliness, feelings of
shame and guilt created by the separation from loved ones, and

ambivalence toward the sociocultural role expectations they face externally and intrapsychically may be considerably intensified by their specific circumstances as "unattached" women. They may retain traditional role expectations for themselves regardless of how unrealistic those might be in the new context. They also may feel free from family control, which can yield the development of more flexible behavior in response to the new culture. Because they are alone and unencumbered by familial expectations, they may acculturate faster to negotiate the varied pressures they encounter in the new environment. In this case, they may face criticism from other immigrants from their home country because of their nonconformity to traditional roles. Both men and women in the immigrant community may show disapproval of unaccompanied women because they may represent a threat to marriage, family, and the community's internal social order. Even though they constitute a numerical minority among immigrants, these women present compelling stories. Their tales will emerge within this text.

Adolescent girls or young women who leave their country without their families may find themselves affected by a premature and traumatic separation from their parents that can stall or delay the process of healthy psychological separation in adulthood (Espín et al., 1990; Rodríguez-Nogués, 1983). In a discussion of immigrants' experiences when returning to their homelands, Paris (1978) likens the forced individuation caused by leaving a parent behind to the impossibility of completing the rapprochement stage in the life of a child. The rapprochement period is characterized by an ambivalence between the desire to return to the mother and a need for distance from her. During this period of development the child plays a continuous game of shadowing mother and darting away from her. In short, Paris argues that in order for an immigrant to successfully complete their individuation and reconciliation with the parents in adulthood, periodic return to parents and homeland is essential. "Emotional refueling" may necessitate periodic returns to the country of birth— what Paris calls a "symbolic return."

For some young immigrant women, particularly refugees, returning is impossible. They may feel cut off from their past history. They rarely have the opportunity to test their newly developed identity, emotional life, and feelings with their birth family.

The impossibility of regular communication with parents prevents the young woman from resolving conflicts that originated before the separation took place. While some similarities exist when parents are deceased, major differences are present in the case of immigrant and refugee women. Living and geographically inaccessible parents can be affected by the woman's present anger or resentment; dead parents cannot. The immigrant woman unable to have regular contact with parents frequently feels guilty about any negative feelings toward them. This is exacerbated if they are in a dangerous situation in their country. A monthly long-distance phone call to an absent mother does little to alleviate problematic issues.

Mothers who are forced by ex-husbands or situational factors to leave their children behind provide another example of women strongly affected by the inability to work out problematic feelings. The feelings of guilt and loss may become accentuated by the lack of contact with their growing children.

In certain instances the refugee is allowed to return to her country of origin for brief visits. Even then, the time needed for resolving familial issues is not available during a brief family re-encounter after years of absence. Moreover, if she is able to have extended visits to her country of origin, the birth family still does not witness the change experienced by the woman in the new country. Dismissal or denial of the important life changes she has experienced is all too easy, increasing the feeling of being cut off from loved ones.

Additional Factors in the Migration Experience

As already mentioned, factors other than gender, such as age, class, and race, affect the process of acculturation and adaptation for women immigrants. Personal demographics largely determine the experience of adaptation. For example, light-skinned, young, middle-class, educated immigrants usually encounter a more favorable reception in the United States than dark-skinned, older, poor, and uneducated newcomers. When an immigrant comes from a country where she belongs to the racial majority (or where racial mixtures are the norm), the experience of being labeled an ethnic or racial minority person in the United States is disconcerting. Encountering overt racial discrimination becomes a disorienting experience. This loss of status creates frustration and tensions often compounded by economic need and lack of fluency in the new language. These factors frequently add to downward mobility in employment, particularly for refugees.

Thus, a significant consequence of the immigrant's transitions is a growing sensation of discontinuity of identity (Garza-Guerrero, 1974). The psychosocial context in which the individual's sense of identity was originally formed has been left behind. Consequently, the individual struggles with reorganizing and reintegrating identity within the new context.

The specific sociopolitical, economic, and historical circumstances that motivated the migration also affect the individual's sense of self and the process of adaptation. Their impact may appear more decisively in women refugees (Cole, Espín, & Rothblum, 1992) than in those who voluntarily migrated, due to the danger surrounding refugees' departure and the impossibility of returning regularly to the country of origin.

If political persecution (e.g., incarceration, torture, or the disappearance of family members) or gender-specific forms of violence (e.g., rape) preceded migration, other unique factors become part of one's adaptation. Women refugees may have been subjected to further harassment and rape or other forms of sexual abuse used as a means of torture at the hands of their "protectors" or "saviors" during their escape from their country of origin. Women thus subjected frequently suffer from posttraumatic stress reactions as a consequence of these events (Figley, 1985; Molesky, 1986). Posttraumatic stress reactions may manifest themselves through nightmares, numbing of feelings, and an overwhelming sense of guilt. Empirical evidence suggests that sadness, depression, and more serious pathologies can recur or develop years after the actual migration took place (e.g., Rodríguez-Nogués, 1983; Telles, 1980).

Certain torture and abuse experiences that refugees may have suffered are inconceivable to many Americans, and the refugee often is made to feel like a liar (Cole, Espín, & Rothblum, 1992). Mental health professionals have observed that just the telling of the experiences, the opportunity to speak the unspeakable, may be therapeutic for these women (Aron, 1992; Cienfuegos & Monelli, 1983; Figley, 1985). For women who have experienced torture and political persecution before migration, giving voice to their experiences and being believed provides an enormous relief and contributes to their healing.

Issues of Loss and Grief

As stated earlier, to understand the experiences of immigrants and refugees, we must focus on loss, grief, and mourning as issues of primary importance. Discussions of the psychological distress experienced by immigrants and refugees emphasize their need to cope with new experiences,—usually defined as "acculturative stress" (Berry & Annis, 1974)—rather than the loss of the old familiar environment implied in the loss of home country and loved ones.

> Losses usually stem from the traumas of the uprooting experience through involuntary or voluntary extraction from the primary group networks in the society of origin. The loss of the social circle composed of intimate face-to-face contact with family, friends and neighbors is pungently distressful. (Rogler, 1994, p. 704)

From a psychological point of view, "[t]he degree of choice or necessity at the time of and preparation for relocation influence the kind of loss that is experienced . . . and play a major role in the kind of mourning process required" (Levy-Warren, 1987, p. 307). Indeed, researchers have observed that the degree of trauma experienced before departure—the context of exit—is a significant predictor of the psychological well-being and future adjustment of the immigrant or refugee (Portes & Rumbaut, 1996).

In his classic study of the human impact of different experiences of loss and change, urban studies scholar Peter Marris described the difficulties in mourning losses brought on by ambivalent experiences such as migration, in which positive and negative outcomes overlap. According to Marris, "loss disrupts our ability to find meaning in experience, and grief represents the struggle to retrieve this sense of meaning when circumstances have bewildered or betrayed it" (1986, p. 147). "Acts of mourning attenuate the leave-taking" (Marris, 1986, p. 84), but most immigrants are expected to be happy that they have succeeded in migrating rather than sad about what they have lost. Sadness and grief are easily perceived by members of the host culture as ingratitude and perhaps as incongruent even by the immigrant herself. Regardless of gratitude for their new country and relief from whatever anxieties were experienced in the home country, the transitions created by immigration demand that one grieves for the old attachments to country and people. Well-meaning but underinformed friends and social service agencies frequently emphasize the woman's adaptation to her new life rather than her feelings of loss. However, feelings of loss and the need to mourn those losses are at the crux of the process of successful adaptation. For healthy adaptation to occur these feelings of loss must become integrated into the individual psyche. But in so doing, identity is unavoidably transformed, and this transformation brings with it the additional need to mourn the old identity.

The loss of some of life's small, taken for granted pleasures may grow to enormous proportions in the emotional life of the immigrant:

> The pain of uprootedness is also activated in subtle forms by the everyday absence of familiar smells, familiar foods, familiar routines for doing the small tasks of daily life. It is the lack of . . . "the average expectable environment" . . . which can become a constant reminder of what is not there anymore. (Espín, 1992, p. 13)

The idealization of the home country increases the feeling of loss. Despite the fact that the migration may have been motivated by less than optimal conditions in the homeland, the unrealistic feeling that one has lost a paradise may persist.

The grieving process involves a moderate level of emotional disorganization. It may manifest as apathy, insomnia, loss of appetite, irritability, angry outbursts, psychosomatic symptoms, and other signs of distress. As Lindemann (1944) argued in his classic study on grief and mourning, when these feelings are inhibited because the loss is denied or otherwise defended against, the normal signs can become pathological by prolongation or exaggeration. Parkes's (1975) seminal study of grief and bereavement suggested several identifiable features of grief and mourning. These include a gradual process from denial to recognition and acceptance; alarm reactions such as anxiety and other related physiological symptoms; an urge to search and find the lost object; anger and guilt; feelings of internal loss of self; and identification with the lost (/love) object.

Although there are similarities between the grief and mourning of bereavement and the losses experienced with migration, the two processes differ in substantial ways.

> The analogy with bereavement does not fit the changes [created by the migration]—because circumstances are too baffling to attach any purpose to them, or because purposes are brought into contradiction by the convergence of different aspects of life. (Marris, 1986, p. 148)

The bereaved's grief can be traced to the nature of the relationship to a specific person, while in migration the lost object is vague and the loss pervasive. Migrants have lost country, culture, and loved ones along with their "average expectable environment" (Hartmann, 1964). All habitual patterns are disrupted while new ones are learned, and the distress can be considerable. Immigrants themselves seldom understand the magnitude of this loss. They and others may miss the extent of the trauma behind a facade of successful adaptation. Telles (1980) observed the effects of delayed grief on middle-aged Cuban women. They experienced reactivated grief when they retired from their jobs after many years of residing in the United States. Their depression and emotional distress were traced directly to their lack of successful mourning years earlier during migration. Rodríguez-Nogués (1983) studied the experience of Cuban women who had migrated to the United States in the early 1960s as unaccompanied minors. Many of these women did not recognize the traumatic consequences of their migration until years later. As adults, they realized how the demands of the traumatic situation they experienced so early in life had forced them to behave beyond their years in order to cope. Twenty years later, they discussed how the special circumstances of their migration had left little room for mourning the loss of parents and country. In the interim, they all apparently had adapted successfully to life in the United States. At the time of the interview, they reflected on the lost parts or their childhood and on the difficulty of being angry or upset with the parents who had sent them away. They had not allowed themselves to feel the losses or the anger because they were aware that their parents had made a great sacrifice deciding to separate from their children to protect them from perceived danger. The mixture of positive and negative feelings involved in migration complicates dramatically the emotional picture of the immigrant.

Again, Marris's analysis provides a perspective on what the contradictory experiences of the immigrant entail:

> A system of values, by its nature, offers a stable frame of reference by which to interpret events. . . . It assigns a consistent ethical meaning. But a set of principles can only be applied to regular happenings, since their interpretation depends upon recognizing the categories into which events fall, and this recognition rests in turn on assimilating the present to past experience. It must be predictable what good behavior should be. (1986, p. 119)

This is precisely the frame of reference that the contrasting values of home and host cultures disrupt, and this "can be most disorienting and most disruptive of the person's previously established identity" (Espín, 1992, p. 13).

Immigrants frequently experience feelings of guilt toward people and relationships left behind. New loyalties in the host country may be experienced as betrayal of the loved ones and the homeland. In other words, "invisible loyalties"—as described by Boszormenyi-Nagy & Spark (1973)—interfere with adapting to the new country. Invisible loyalties can be emotionally paralyzing and induce compulsive behavior in individuals and families.

Indeed, the immigrant's "sense of their own identity may be profoundly disturbed, if they feel that adaptation requires them to betray their earlier attachments" (Marris, 1986, p. 82).

To compensate for these losses and grief feelings, many immigrants struggle to maintain contact with the home country. They do this through food, music, physical proximity, and contact with other immigrants from the home country. That is why the presence of co-ethnics and a sense of cultural heritage has been found to be positively related to mental health and well-being among immigrants (Portes & Rumbaut, 1996). Sometimes the immigrant must return to the homeland in order to realize what the losses had entailed (Espín, 1992).

The Importance of "Place"

Obviously, geography is of critical importance to immigrants. The *place* in which events occur is of paramount importance. The immigrant's life preoccupations are frequently focused on the vicissitudes of place and geography (Espín, 1992, 1994b, 1995, 1996c, 1997). This preoccupation has two components. First, whatever events may be occurring at a distance in the country of origin give it a sense of unreality despite—or precisely because of—its constant psychological presence for the immigrant. This I interpret as a manifestation of Parkes's (1975) "urge to search for and find the lost [and love] object" that we discussed earlier. The other I identify as a preoccupation with "what could have been." Preoccupation with what could have been if the women had not left their countries is a central theme in their emotional lives. This manifests as ruminations about what life might have entailed if the immigrant had remained in her homeland or migrated to a different country, or if the immigration had taken place at another life stage. This preoccupation is expressed in two ways: First, the immigrant asks what could have happened in her life had she stayed in her country of origin. Then her concern shifts to ask what has been gained by the migration. My own reflections on my exodus following a return to my homeland after many years reflect these preoccupations:

> My trip made me realize that my memories had a geography. . . . That my country, in fact, exists beyond what I think or feel or remember about her. . . . [B]efore my return I never knew that I felt as if my country did not have a real existence beyond my memory. (Espín, 1992, p. 16)

In a more interpersonal realm,

> My trip put me in touch with childhood friends and made me reflect about the differences in our lives, about the choices to stay or leave that have dramatically influenced our life projects. None of us has any way of knowing what our lives would have been like without the historical dislocations that have marked them. . . . It is impossible to know if our decisions have resulted in a better life project for any of us, although we each hope and believe to have made the best decision. (Espín, 1992, p. 17)

One researcher has characterized these ruminations by describing how "the migration experience creates an emergent phenomenology of incessant reference group comparisons and trade-offs between the benefits of the host society and the losses incurred in departing from the society of origin" (Rogler, 1994, p. 704). Cuban American writer Achy Obejas, describing her own ruminations about her migration, illustrated these concerns and their relationship to sexuality in a recent autobiographical story. She pondered,

> What if we'd stayed? What if we'd never left Cuba? . . . I
> wonder, if we'd stayed then who, if anyone, would have been
> my blond lovers, or any kind of lovers at all. . . . I try to imag-
> ine who I would have been . . . but I can't. I can only think of
> variations of who I am, not who I might have been. (1994,
> pp. 124–125).

Psychologist Albert Bandura (1982) argues that chance encounters
have a profound effect on the course of human development and life
paths. He believes that "a comprehensive developmental theory must
specify factors that set and alter particular life courses if it is to
provide an adequate explanation of human behavior" (p. 747). For
some people, chance encounters are compounded by historical and
political events beyond their control (e.g., Espín, 1987b). People
subjected to historical dislocations feel these changes as more
intrapsychically drastic and dramatic than the average person who
has not shared these experiences (Espín, 1992).

Conclusion

This chapter highlighted the stress created by migration. Emphasis
was placed on emotionally conflictual situations, yet most of the reactions discussed in this chapter are not pathological, even though
some women immigrants may present pathological manifestations of
the stress. The sources of these possible pathological manifestations
are usually found in the personal history prior to relocation. Other
traumatic events experienced earlier in life are easily exacerbated by
the stresses of migration. However, the vast majority of women
immigrants and refugees navigate these stresses and grow from the
lessons learned to become healthy, productive members of society.
The life narratives included in this book provide examples of women
immigrants' many variations of successful adaptation to their new life
in a new country.

Notes

1. Gender-specific forms of persecution such as genital mutilation, forced prostitution, and rape (as an instrument of politically motivated torture and domination) have begun to attract attention from the United Nations and in U.S. courts.
2. Although this may be true also for nonimmigrant adolescent girls in the United States, the conflict for immigrant girls is colored by their desire to "become American" and their parents' fears of what this might entail.

2 | Collecting Immigrant Women's Life Narratives

Life Narrative as Psychological Research Method

In the last half century psychological research has been dominated by research methods that isolate characteristics and behaviors for study through experimental and statistical procedures. This approach judges the use of narrative for research as "subjective" and thus "unscientific." While other social sciences have used narratives to understand human life, there is a contradiction within psychology in relation to the credibility of the use of narratives as psychological data. On the one hand, there is a tradition of using narratives for research in psychology. This is particularly true in the field of personality psychology. (See for example, some classic works in the field such as Murray, 1938, *Explorations in Personality*; Allport, 1942, *The Use of Personal Documents in Psychological Science*; and White, 1966, *Lives in Progress*.) In addition, the whole field of psychotherapy, beginning with Freud, is based on the use of narrative. Psychotherapy is a reconstruction of the life story. One tells one's story to a sympathetic listener. In the process of being listened to and responded to in a new way, one's story and one's habitual modes of reaction take on reinterpreted meaning, and as a consequence become assumed and incorporated in a different way. Diagnosis is nothing but a way of organizing a narrative and making sense of disparate symptoms and experiences. On the other hand, because of the emphasis on "scientific objectivity" that has characterized psychology in the last half century, even psychotherapy, in an effort to appear "scientific," has looked for categories that would legitimize its processes. Freud himself developed categories such as id, ego, super-ego, transference, libido, and so on, that reified the narratives and life stories on which he based his theories.

Presently, a renewed interest in the use of other, more qualitative methods is emerging within psychology (e.g., Smith, Harré, & Van Langenhove, 1995). There is a renewed interest in "the role of narrative in establishing personal identity" (Polkinghorne, 1988, p. 105). This is predicated on the idea that a self needs a story in order "to be." Erikson (1975) spoke about the individuals' emotional need to reconstruct life through narrative so that it looks planned. McAdams studied the role of narrative in "binding together our lives in time" (1990, p. 166). These authors and others (e.g., Josselson & Lieblich, 1993; Sarbin, 1986) emphasize the importance of using narratives for research in psychology. In particular, they address how "narratives construct and transform the passing of life into a coherent self" (Polkinghorne, 1988, p. 119).

As Rosenwald (1988) has observed, "psychologists have generally neglected the detailed study of lives because it has not seemed to contribute to the formulation of general truths" (p. 239). Psychology has neglected a very significant source of data by denying the potential of life narratives for understanding the inner structure of social and psychological phenomena. This omission has contributed to a "fundamental attribution error—the common misperception of social problems as individual ones" (Rosenwald, 1988, p. 242). The reality is that "social conditions bring about and shape phenomena that individuals regard as . . . private and . . .

unique" (Rosenwald, 1988, p. 242), but that are actually part of the collective experience.

As some theorists recently have argued, "cultures provide specific plots for lives" (Polkinghorne, 1988, p. 153; Rosenwald & Ochberg, 1992). To create a life plot, "social ideology [is] individually appropriated in the construction of life histories and selves" (Rosenwald & Ochberg, 1992, p. 5). That is the reason why "certain kinds of stories can only be told at particular social moments" (Plummer, 1995, p. 167).

As psychologist George Rosenwald (1992) theorized:

> When people tell life stories, they do so in accordance with models of intelligibility specific to the culture. . . . Not only acceptable behavior, but also acceptable accounts of behavior are socialized. . . . Accounts bind individuals to the arrangements of the society enforcing the models. (p. 265)

In short, stories and lives develop through compromise between the individual's desires and stabilizing societal influences. These two forces balance each other or push each other's limits. As Ochberg (1992) argued, "the tales we tell each other [and ourselves] about who we are and might yet become are individual variations on the narrative templates our culture deems intelligible" (p. 214). Scholars of life narratives point to this interplay. A process occurs: The culture speaks through the individual narrator and provides that individual with the needed support to live, develop, and feel "normal." Indeed, even models of "craziness" must meet culturally acceptable standards.

The use of life narrative is a particularly valuable research method when the concepts being explored are "new territory" for participants and/or researcher (Mishler, 1986; Riessman, 1993). In addition to its value as a research tool (e.g., Denzin, 1989; Gagnon, 1992; Josselson & Lieblich, 1993; Riessman, 1993), retelling the life story, including the migration (particularly if it was motivated by some form of persecution), has been shown to have a healing effect (Aron, 1992; Cienfuegos & Monelli, 1983).

Narrative, Psychology, and Migration

Surely we agree that culture and history are powerful forces in human development. What, then, happens when the cultural narrative changes abruptly as it does through migration? How is one's individual life, sense of self, and life story altered? Although "the story about life is open to editing and revision" (Polkinghorne, 1988, p. 154), some life-altering events may require more intensive revisions of the "plot" than others. "Rewriting one's story involves major life changes" (Polkinghorne, 1988, p. 182). Sometimes major life changes demand the rewriting of one's story. Events that happen out in the world are not only social, but psychological as well (e.g., revolutions, wars, migration, peace accords, plagues, earthquakes, or other political events and natural phenomena). These events help shape individual psychological structure as well as societal directions. Some of these events disrupt individual lives for days and weeks; others entirely change one's life course. These events transform the cultural plots of the expectable and the ensuing social context. Sometimes this occurs because the culture itself is transformed. In other instances, the individual finds herself in a new cultural context that allows for telling a different kind of story. Some classical studies of life history have their genesis in these cataclysms (e.g., Thomas & Znaniecki, 1918–1920/1927). Increased understanding and knowledge about other social transformations have also benefited from narrative approaches. For example, feminist studies of women's life stories have recently been included in this genre (e.g., Franz & Stewart, 1994).

Hazards of Narrative Studies

One of the objections raised against the use of narratives in research is that one needs to be mindful of the trustworthiness of interviewees. Yet it is equally important in studies with sensitive topics—regardless of method—to be aware that the information is being developed in a context of intersubjectivity.

Researchers and researched mutually influence each other and the quality of the data. Feminist scholarship has challenged traditional research methodology and its myth of objectivity. This has been one of feminism's most valuable contributions to psychology and to other disciplines. Feminist researchers have emphasized that "the very fact that a researcher poses a particular question can have major social implications even if the research is never performed" (Renzetti & Lee, 1993, p. 27). "Central to [the feminist] critique has been the debunking of the myth of value-free scientific inquiry" (Renzetti & Lee, 1993, p. 177). Instead, an acknowledgment is made of the researcher's and the participants' cross-fertilizing effects.

When the researcher's experiences share characteristics with those of the researched—as in this book—trust may be increased. This may result in more easily forthcoming "truth." By the same token, similar experiences may create a sense of competition in the research participants. They may try to measure up to the imagined expectations of a researcher who has shared similar experiences.

Conversely, the interview process may be impaired by the research participants' belief that they need to protect themselves from outsiders. This may be particularly true in the case of women immigrants, who by definition are in a less powerful position in society.

In narrative studies, the researcher cannot forget that

> story telling flows in a stream of power. . . . Power is a
> process that weaves its way through embodied passionate
> social life and everything in its wake. Sexual stories [as stories
> of intimate family relationships] live in this flow of power.
> The power to tell a story, or indeed to not tell a story, under
> the conditions of one's own choosing [is part of this process].
> (Plummer, 1995, p. 26)

The women interviewed herein were all volunteers. They had no reason compelling them to participate except their own desire and willingness. I am confident that the bulk of the life narratives contain honest information. Yet, as with all narrative, one needs to keep in mind that

> whatever else a story is, it is not simply the lived life. It speaks
> all around the life . . .[and] suggests links between a life and a

> culture ...[which brings us again to] ... the socially
> constructed nature of the story telling process. (Plummer,
> 1995, pp. 168–169)

My Research on Immigrant Women

The research presented in this book expands on my earlier work. It seeks to make a contribution to the development of narrative research in psychology and to understanding women's lives through feminist analysis. My goal has been to value and transmit the immigrant and refugee women's voices. Their narratives capture and present their own intimate lives through their stories.

The studies reported in this book sought to increase knowledge and understanding of the experience of migration. They also focus especially on sexuality and gender-related issues among immigrant and refugee women. The narratives illuminate women's sexual expressions and experiences in different cultures. These are created by disparate social forces that include relationships between generations of women affected by migration and the varied experiences of adolescents and adult women. Through this methodology, previously silenced experiences are given voice in intimate life stories.

The narratives presented in Chapter 3 explore immigrant women's understanding of their lives and their sexuality. They also explicate their internalized cultural norms. The open-ended narratives allowed the interviewees to express thoughts and feelings. The format also invited participants to introduce their own themes and concerns. These stories

> must be seen to be socially produced in social contexts by embodied concrete people experiencing the thoughts and feelings of everyday life. ... If these stories are "texts," then they are the texts embodied by breathing passionate people in the full stream of social life. ... Personal and sexual stories ... make a difference: a difference to our lives, our communities, our cultures, our politics. (Plummer, 1995, p. 16)

My study of immigrant women's sexuality has a primary descriptive and explanatory dimension. However, in keeping with much research using life narratives, it is also likely when using these methods to witness another more "therapeutic" dimension of the research. Obviously, the research itself is not therapy. It is intended as a fact-finding and interpretation-identifying enterprise. But it has also been shown to have a side effect as a therapeutic or healing process for those participants traumatized by historical events. Specifically, it helps them reconstruct their life experiences and the dislocation created by sociopolitical events. This is followed by the reintegration of these experiences into their own self-understanding of their life course. The three studies reported in this book sought these positive effects for the participants.

I have witnessed that focus groups and individual interviews encourage participants to get in touch with these experiences and reintegrate them in their life narratives. Participating adolescents had the opportunity to air their problematic experiences as they struggled to interweave adolescent identity, immigrant status, and acculturation. The mother-daughter study participants spoke about feelings seldom discussed. Women in the study of immigrant sexuality and gender roles spoke about intimate matters crucial to their lives. These included identities, sense of self, and "taboo" subjects in everyday life.

It is the researcher's ethical responsibility to ensure that study procedures protect participants from the damaging reactions caused by recalling traumatic experiences. Ethical considerations are important in all research. Yet these issues are foregrounded poignantly when the research topic is personal. In the studies reported herein, they include sensitive topics that are rarely the subject of everyday conversations (Bakan, 1996; Josselson, 1996; Renzetti & Lee, 1993).

Approaches to Data Collection and Analysis

Most of the life narratives included herein were collected through individual interviews. Others were collected through focus groups. An explanatory word on each approach is in order.

As one researcher explained, "the focus group interview is a qualitative research technique used to obtain data about feelings and opinions of small groups of participants about a given problem, experience or other phenomenon" (Basch, 1987, p. 414). Focus groups provide the opportunity to interview a group of people on a particular topic. This form of in-depth interviewing is effective and economical in terms of time and money. It is a pragmatic approach for a study done with limited funds and personnel. Focus groups follow basic principles of qualitative research. They take advantage of the additional information generated through group interaction. They provide the researcher with additional flexibility because they probe unanticipated areas that may have been overlooked when designing the discussion questions (Krueger, 1994; Morgan, 1988, 1993; Stewart & Shamdasani, 1990).

"Qualitative interviewing is a way of finding out what others feel and think about their worlds" (Rubin & Rubin, 1995, p. 1). It is based on conversation, a basic mode of human interaction—but it is a very unique form of conversation, intended as information gathering (Kvale, 1996). The approach used in the studies was semistructured life narrative interviewing focused on specific topics. The purpose of this approach and the interviews was "to obtain descriptions of the life world of the interviewee with respect to interpreting the meaning of the described phenomena" (Kvale, 1996, p. 6). "The qualitative research interview is a construction site of knowledge" (Kvale, 1996, p. 42). This knowledge is constructed in an interrelational context in which the person narrates her story in a conversation with a stranger (Weiss, 1994). "The medium of the interview is language. . . . The focus on language shifts attention away from the notion of an objective reality [because] language constitutes reality [and] each language constructs reality in its own way" (Kvale, 1996, p. 43).

Particularly important is the role of language when interviewing people whose first language is not be the language in which the interview is conducted.

> In interview research, language is both the tool of interviewing and, in the form of tapes and transcripts, also the object

of textual interpretation. Nevertheless, it has been rare in the social sciences for interview researchers to analyze the language medium they use as tools for and objects of their research. (Kvale, 1996, p. 43)

The issue of language—the language of the interview and the language preferred by bilingual individuals to discuss specific topics—will be discussed in Chapter 5.

Focus groups and individual interview topics cover a wide range of concerns. The issues include menstruation; arranged marriages versus dating; marrying outside one's ethnic group; lesbianism and bisexuality; sex and romance; heterosexual intercourse; sex education in the schools and at home; family violence; rape; mothers' passivity versus active involvement in their daughters' lives; and surrounding sexual issues in each family.

In the two formats, I explored ways in which women's sexual behavior signified the family's value system. This means exploring ways in which immigrant and refugee families' conflicts and struggles center on issues of daughters' sexual behaviors and women's sex roles. The two interview formats have allowed me to explore the participants' vocabulary of sex in different languages. Specifically, I have explored variations in the speakers' comfort (or discomfort) when addressing sexuality and what is permissible to say about it in the mother tongue or in English.

Two of the focus groups were comprised of native speakers of the same language (in one case, German; in the other, Spanish). The participants in these two groups came from the same cultural background. A third group included women from several different countries speaking different first languages. I facilitated and conducted all focus groups and interviews included in the main study. For Spanish- and French-speaking participants, I offered to conduct the groups and individual interviews in their mother tongue. Eventually, the Spanish speakers' group was conducted in English and Spanish, because I was able to switch between those two languages. The other two groups were conducted in English because participants spoke languages I cannot speak. When Spanish- or French- speaking participants preferred to be interviewed in English, their request was honored. The request itself was considered data. For participants whose first language I cannot speak, careful questioning about vocabulary in their language was pursued. I also asked questions about the effect of conducting the interview in either English, Spanish, or French. Their responses were incorporated into the discussions.

Description of Participants

Numerical and graphic summaries of the demographic data concerning the participants detail their salient characteristics. The women interviewed are not representative of any universe or population of immigrant women; the demographics presented are meant as descriptors of the characteristics of this group of women only. They are not representative of immigrant women in the United States in general.

Immigrant and refugee women were recruited through personal contacts and friendship pyramiding (which often are called "snowballing" techniques: one participant leads to another). In a few cases, women approached me offering and requesting to be interviewed. Obviously, these participants do not represent all the immigrant and refugee women of the world. Nor do they represent the proportions of different groups, countries, languages, or sexual orientations worldwide. Hence these studies cannot be taken as estimates of any particular group, country, language, or sexual orientation among the immigrant population. They are compelling examples of 43 women's unique life paths.

The objection could be raised that these women are not "typical" immigrants because they are all highly educated and fluent in English. This reveals the misconception that the typical immigrant is poor, uneducated, and unable to communicate in English. The reality is that immigrants to the United States, particularly after 1965, come from all social classes in their countries of origin and adapt to the host society in a variety of ways, including becoming successful and highly educated. Although many immigrants come from deprived economic backgrounds and find employment in the United States only at the bottom of the occupational ladder, others do not. "Neither sweatshops nor poor working conditions have disappeared [for immigrant women]" (Gabaccia, 1994, p. 55). However, "not all immigrants left lives of poverty and hardship [in their countries of birth]; not all started at the bottom of the U.S. economy or remained there, struggling in poverty all their lives" (Gabaccia, 1994, p. 96). Regardless of their social standing in their country of birth, as they adapt to life in the United States, some may experience downward mobility while others may flourish. In any case, there is no typical immigrant because there are multiple differences among immigrants. The image of the typical immigrant woman may be nothing more than a stereotype.

Most importantly, these studies necessitated the recruitment of women able to articulate their experiences cogently in English. The purpose and design of the studies precluded the selection of those unable to communicate in English or to describe and analyze their experiences as speakers of more than one language. This choice of participants does not preclude the possibility that other women immigrants may have different experiences; conversely, it provides a picture of the hardships immigration entails for all women who have migrated, even for those individuals who eventually adjusted successfully and prospered in American society.

A statistical sampling of the characteristics of the universe of immigrant women can be approached from a different methodological perspective. By definition, life narrative research focuses on the personal rather than the collective. The development of knowledge in narrative research is not "accomplished by setting aside subjective factors, but by focusing on them intensively. [Interviewees] are not considered interchangeable: Because each contributes [her] own distinctive appreciation of the totality, [her] 'viewpoint' is indispensable" (Rosenwald, 1988, p. 246). Even though not every single viewpoint can be included, "the synthesis [of immigrant women's experiences] is sculpted in a series of approximations" (Rosenwald, 1988, p. 256). The viewpoints presented in this book enrich the picture of women immigrants and contribute to dispelling myths about them.

The presentation of figures is not meant to detract or compromise the value of their narratives. Rather, the data provide the reader with a picture of these women as a group. In Chapter 3 summaries of the 43 women's narratives are presented.

Table 1

Code Name	Location of Interview	Age at Interview	Age at Migration	Period of Migration	Region of Origin
Marguerite	Southern California	29	27	1990s	Europe
Hilde	Southern California	28	26	1990s	Europe
Ursula	Southern California	30	19	1980s	Europe
Angela	Southern California	33	Unknown	1960s	Latin America
Leticia	Southern California	41	17	1970s	Latin America
Sandra	Southern California	26	Unknown	1970s	Latin America
Inge	Southern California	45	27	1960s	Europe
Jazmin	Southern California	31	14	1970s	Asia
Sudha	Southern California	23	Unknown	1970s	South Asia
Sissy	Southern California	23	4	1970s	Asia
Denise	Southern California	61	30	1970s	Canada
Sylvia	Southern California	30	9	1970s	Caribbean
Kerine	Southern California	28	12	1970s	Caribbean
Noriko	Southern California	33	30	1970s	Asia
Judith	Midwest	75	11	1930s	Europe
Lorena	Northeast	47	30	1970s	Latin America
Cindy	Northeast	42	2	1950s	Asia
Liv	Northwest	69	13	1930s	Europe
Manel	Northwest	24	20	1990s	South Asia
Lin	Northwest	27	12	1980s	Asia
Mei	Northwest	40	12	1950s	Asia
Maya	Northwest	51	35	1970s	Europe
Maritza	Southeast	42	22	1970s	Latin America
Olga	Southeast	54	22	1960s	Latin America
Aurelia	Northern California	31	13	1980s	Asia
Shelo	Northern California	26	18	1980s	Asia
Ayla	Northern California	40	29	1980s	Middle East
Soledad	Northern California	32	13	1980s	Latin America
Cecilia	Northern California	60	19	1950s	Latin America
Rosa	Northern California	32	12	1970s	Latin America
Cornelia	Northern California	30	26	1990s	Latin America
Lucia	Northern California	40	9	1960s	Latin America
Rivka	Northeast	70	12	1930s	Europe
Marie-Claire	Northeast	31	11	1970s	Caribbean
Eva	Northeast	41	20	1970s	Europe

Thirty-five immigrant and refugee women were interviewed between 1993 and 1995 for the study on the transformation of sexuality and gender roles. Table 1 summarizes the characteristics of the women included in this group, including: location of (individual or group) interview; age at the time of the interview; age at migration; decade when the migration took place; and region of origin.

The interviews for this study took place in several cities in the United States: San Diego, California; Chicago, Illinois; Miami, Florida; San Francisco, California; Seattle, Washington; Boston, Massachusetts; and New York, New York. All focus groups were held in San Diego. The choice of these cities was determined by two factors. One was the possibility of accessing a wider variety of cultures and countries of origin and populations by recruiting prospective participants in several regions of the United States. The cities chosen for the study have a rich ethnically and racially mixed population of immigrants and refugees. These sites complement each other because they represent geographical and ethnic diversity within the United States. The second reason was pragmatic: Personal plans and professional connections facilitated my travel and access to these cities.

The interviews for the other two studies were conducted mostly in the Northeast. There was one participant from the Southeast and another from Southern California. Table 2 provides information on the participants in the mother-daughter study whose stories are presented herein. Table 3 provides the same information on the participants from the adolescence and migration study.

The charts provide information on all 43 interviewees' characteristics. As shown in Figure 1, 34.9% of interviews (for a total of 15

Table 2

Code Name	Location of Interview	Age at Interview	Age at Migration	Period of Migration	Region of Origin
Roya	Northeast	23	16	1980s	Middle East
Mina	Northeast	28	24	1980s	Middle East
Violeta	Northeast	51	22	1960s	Latin America
Colleen	Northeast	61	14	1960s	Europe
Nora	Southeast	60	17	1950s	Latin America
Annette	Southern California	52	19	1950s	Europe

Table 3

Code Name	Location of Interview	Age at Interview	Age at Migration	Period of Migration	Region of Origin
Novena	Northeast	17	13	1980s	Europe
Iris	Northeast	17	14	1980s	Middle East

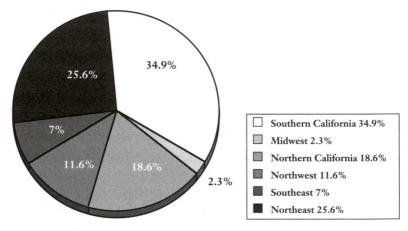

Figure 1   Region of Interview
(Figures reflect all participants)

interviews) took place in Southern California, 25.6% (or 11 inter-views) in the Northeast, 18.6% (or 8 interviews) in Northern California, 11.6% (or 5 interviews) in the Northwest, 7% (or 3 inter-views) in the Southeast, and 2.3% (or 1 interview) in the Midwest.

Figure 2 presents the ages of participants at the time of the inter-view. A fourth of the participants (25.6% of the 43 women) were between the ages of 20 and 29. A similar number of participants (23.3%) were between the ages of 30 and 39. Another 23.3% were between the ages of 40 and 49 at the time of the interview. A smaller number of women were between the ages of 50 and 59 (9.3%) and between the ages of 60 and 69 (also 9.3%), and the smallest number were under the age of 20 (4.7%) and between 70 and 79 (also 4.7%). The age diversity of respondents enriches the picture by providing unique insights germaine to their life cycles' perspective.

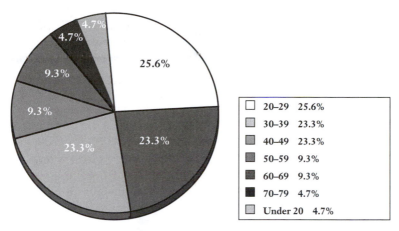

Figure 2   Age at Interview

As shown in Figure 3, the majority of the women migrated between the ages of 11 and 14 (34.9%). A small number, constituting 9.3% of the women interviewed, migrated before the age of 10, thus bringing the percentage of those who had migrated in childhood or early adolescence and puberty to 44.2% of the total. Information on age at migration is unknown for three of the women. The rest of the participants (48.9%) migrated in late adolescence (16.3%) or during adulthood (32.6%).

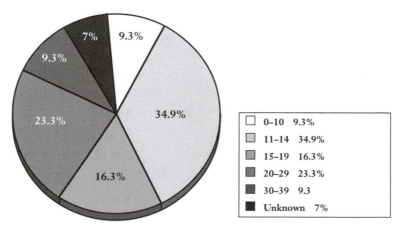

Figure 3   Age at Migration

Figure 4 shows that about half of the women (42.4%) migrated in the 1970s (12.1%) and 1980s (30.3%). While 21.2% migrated in the 1960s and 15.2% in the 1950s, none of the women migrated during the 1940s. Some (12.1%) had just migrated before the interview in the early 1990s. The three oldest women in the study (9.1%) migrated during the 1930s, in the years before World War II.

Several regions of the world were represented by the interviewees. As shown in Figure 5, most of the interviewees migrated from either Latin America (30.2%) or Europe (27.9%). Asian women constituted

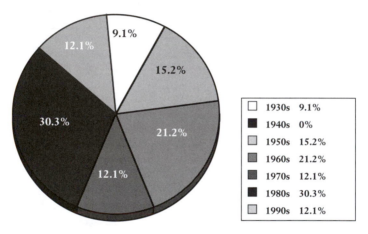

☐	1930s	9.1%
■	1940s	0%
☐	1950s	15.2%
■	1960s	21.2%
■	1970s	12.1%
■	1980s	30.3%
☐	1990s	12.1%

Figure 4 Decade of Migration

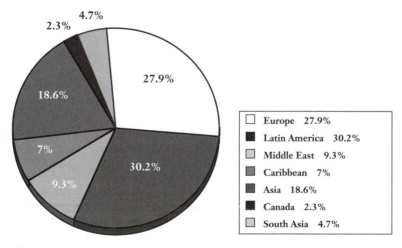

☐	Europe 27.9%
■	Latin America 30.2%
☐	Middle East 9.3%
■	Caribbean 7%
■	Asia 18.6%
■	Canada 2.3%
☐	South Asia 4.7%

Figure 5 Region of Origin

18.6% of the interviewees. In addition, 4.7% came from South Asia (the Indian subcontinent and surrounding area) and 9.3% originated from the Middle East. One of the interviewees was Canadian (2.3%).

As shown in Figure 6, women who identified as lesbian constituted 30.2% of the women interviewed while 69.8% self-defined as heterosexual. This wide representation of lesbian experiences from different countries provides one of the book's unique features, since samples of lesbians are rarely included in studies of women immigrants. Although lesbians are present in all groups of women, most researchers proceed as if all women immigrants are heterosexuals. This false assumption is sustained by silences surrounding the issue. A discussion of the specific experience of lesbian immigrants is included in Chapter 7. Their stories are included in Chapter 3.

Interviews and focus groups were taped, transcribed, and analyzed following accepted techniques for the analysis of qualitative data (e.g., Rubin & Rubin, 1995; Silverman, 1993; Strauss, 1987; Weiss, 1994). Qualitative researchers have observed that "there is no single tried and true method of analysis or strategy for presentation of findings" (Weiss, 1994, p. 152). However, "despite variation in style, all good reports are similar: they tell a coherent story" (Weiss, 1994, p. 153). The rich material provided by the interviewees left me with

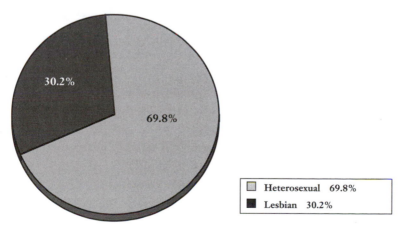

Figure 6   Sexual Orientation

"the typical problem of a narrative researcher: namely, how to extract a narrative from a stretch of discourse" (Mishler, 1995, p. 95). Thus, in analyzing and presenting the data, I have kept the information issue-focused rather than digressing into unrelated forays.

> Both participants and I as the analyst were engaged in acts of reconstruction. They selected some events to report and omitted others . . . because some events may have been excluded and others reframed . . . the told has been constructed in the telling. (Mishler, 1995, p. 96)

What follows in the next chapter is a summary of the forty-three women's life narratives. As is customary in qualitative research, all names are pseudonyms.

3 | The Stories

This chapter presents brief summaries of the life stories of the immigrant and refugee women in the three studies. Only information directly relevant to the topics outlined in the studies are reported in the vignettes. Stories are recounted through the women's own words and my own paraphrasing. Relevant verbatim quotes illustrate and describe each woman's point of view as well as the points under study.

Because the main study addressed issues of cultural identity, sexuality, and sexual identity, the stories told by women in this study focus on those topics. Some participants dwelled more on the experience of migration and on questions of national identity; others gave more extensive answers to the sexuality and sexual identity questions. The other two studies emphasized the effect of migration on the mother-daughter relationship and adolescent development. Consequently, women interviewed for those studies placed more emphasis on those two issues. Most respondents addressed all of these issues to a varying degree.

Regardless of the focus of the studies, each woman's reasons for migration was different. The reasons for migration included the political and economic conditions in the country of birth; the specific motivating circumstances in her life (such as marriage, jobs, desires for family reunification); or a desire for a new life. The respondents vary in their degree of articulation and introspection; thus, some narratives are longer and more detailed than others. It is likely some had reflected about the topics before the interview occurred.

As explained in Chapter 2, the initial data for the main study were gathered through focus group interviews. Later interviews for that study were done individually (as were the interviews in the other two projects). The participants and their stories will be presented in the order in which the interviews occurred. However, some are grouped by nationality or themes (e.g., Latin Americans, lesbians) to facilitate comparisons. This illuminates the recurring themes and issues presented by women sharing common cultural or personal experiences. The presentation of the stories begins, then, with the first three women interviewed for the study and they continue from there.

I interviewed Marguerite, Hilde, and Ursula together in the first focus group. They are native speakers of German and, although I do not speak German, I interviewed them together to observe interactions among them in their own language. They knew each other before the group meeting, and I had had separate interactions with each of them; thus, we were not strangers to each other before the group session. All three were in their late 20s or early 30s. Ursula and Hilde were born in Germany; Marguerite was born in Austria. The three of them lived all their lives in their birth countries before coming to the United States. Hilde and Marguerite had arrived in the United States just two years before, while Ursula had already been in this country for ten years when the interview took place. Ursula, a health professional, defined herself as a lesbian. Marguerite and Hilde hold research jobs and define themselves as heterosexual.

Before the group started, they spoke to each other in German with a few words of English mixed in. When I came into the room they switched to English. I explained again my study's purpose. My opening words were: "As you know, I am interested in women's experience of their own sexuality and how that relates to their cultural background. So, let's start with when, where, and from whom did you get information about sex, sexuality, being a woman, menstruation, and so on. I don't have any particular process to follow. And if there is anything you are interested in, or you think is important, feel free to talk about it."

After that, throughout the three hours of the group discussion, I infrequently interjected some comments or questions.

Their responses revealed similar perspectives and experiences. For example, none of their mothers had said much about sex or even menstruation. Reasonably, Marguerite and Hilde focused more on their experiences growing up in their countries of birth while Ursula referred more to her life in the United States in addition to describing her experiences of growing up in Germany. Marguerite and Hilde came to this country as adults, and had sought jobs that were personally and financially rewarding. They did not leave their countries out of financial, material, or political need. Rather, their motivation was living on their own, without their families, away from the familiar environment. Thus, they did not have any of the typical pressures experienced by other immigrant women, and their comments focused almost exclusively on their lives growing up in their families in their birth country rather than on their experiences of adaptation to the United States. They had a lot to say about growing up as women in their countries and families.

MARGUERITE

Marguerite is the oldest of six children, with four sisters and a brother. She comes from a middle-class family from Austria's rural bourgeoisie. Her family's house and land have been their property for several centuries.

Marguerite started the group's conversation. She described her mother's silences about all sexually related issues (e.g., menstruation):

> my mother kept an eye on me when she assumed I was going to have my first moon, but all her explanations were rather "technical," there was never anything about love. She gave me some tampons and explained a little but not too much, she just gave them to me and said that maybe I'll need them soon. Other than that my friends and cousins told me that babies grow in the mom.

Her use of the word "moon" referred to her period. This was not an Austrian expression, but was one she had learned in this country from Native American women she had met. In general, being in the United States has allowed her to talk about sexual issues. In Austria, this was taboo:

> The region where I come from is very very Catholic. . . . Maybe it is a combination of this Catholicism and a certain agricultural culture that has created a very rigid behavior with regard to sexuality, especially for women. So, for example, where I grew up, in a farm, I never saw anybody naked. Therefore, I am very unfree. And I notice this difference between me and women from Germany. Men in Austria, they can't really deal with women, they are not good lovers.

Marguerite attributed her changing sense of self to her new environment:

> I'm not sure if it is being in America or just being a distance from Austria but I feel I am being affected by this atmosphere that gives me some freedom to experience myself and to be more clear about what's going on with myself. But I definitely feel something changing. The change is in general but also about sexuality. And it is very important for me that it is about sexuality because I was so oppressed there.

She also noted the greater degree of "feminist discussions amongst women in the United States." She contrasted this with an experience she had had in Austria when a boss started sexually harassing her. Her female kinfolk would just laugh about her concern and thought that she should feel flattered rather than upset. She noted that "because women talk about these things here, the conversation changes the consciousness even if they don't know it."

In Austria, Marguerite observed that "sexuality is defined as heterosexual behavior." Because of this emphasis on heterosexuality she noticed more sexual tension under the surface. It's more similar to Italy, flirting all the time. . . .There is a culture of flirting and sexual tension but no language for women to communicate with each other or to help each other, particularly women from different generations.

She lacked women in whom to confide. Sexual relations with men are also impaired by poor communication. "There is a lot of insinuation before but once you are in bed," she noted, "you don't know what you need to be pleased and he doesn't know what to do."

Marguerite reflected on her mother's contradictory messages about women's roles and sexuality. She expressed her frustration with these contradictions and was deeply emotional about these topics.

> My mother wants me to be a virgin until I marry but on the other hand there are all these suggestions and these "fiestas" and this flirting that she encourages. While the Austrian male ski instructor is allowed a "lover-boy" image . . . there is no stereotype for sexy Austrian women because there is this ideal of being a virgin and behaving in very proper ways.

Ironically, she noted, there is a very high rate of illegitimate children in Austria. Meanwhile, women like her mother relentlessly emphasize maintenance of virginity and the use of sexual manipulation over men to exert a modicum of control.

Marguerite elaborated on the hidden violence toward women and the blunting of expressions of sexuality that these contradictory messages breed. She said that there is "a lot of violence, a lot of shouting behind the silence, even though there was no open violence, no beating or slapping." The result, for her, was that

> I was injured in my sexuality. When I hear about African women being circumcised, sometimes I think of myself as being circumcised without being circumcised. Nothing was done to me physically but it was done emotionally.

Cultural taboos, including silence amongst women, kept her from experiencing orgasm until recently. Her female kin, she believes, were similarly denied.

As a child, she learned that sexuality is a place "protected by monsters":

> I don't know how they did it. I only know the results. I even remember taking baths with my sister at 6 or 7 and we did not look at each other: We sat in the same bathtub with our backs to each other.

Marguerite emphasized the importance for women across generations to bond together to protect each other from these pressures.

> It's hard that women don't protect each other. They just don't. Mothers and sisters just can't when something is going on. It is more important to hide everything, to keep the image of the good family or of being the nice person. That is more important than to protect the feelings or the health of other women.

Marguerite is painfully aware of the poignant contradictions in women's roles. Her mother instructed her and her sisters to go to the kitchen to do dishes after dinner while excusing her brother. But at the same time she has taught them not to take their father or other men seriously:

> She doesn't take him very seriously. And that is an important message. I have a hard time taking men seriously. Women are caring for everything, women are strong, they are in the background but they are running everything. And men are kind of . . . well you can't take them seriously. I learned to feel superior in certain respects. I think I learned this being rigid and being in charge of everything and to be afraid of sexuality from my mother.

Marguerite was unaware of lesbianism when she was growing up. She became conscious of it when a teenager friend came out at age 19. While she shared in the excitement of her friend's discovery, they soon parted as they gravitated to different groups of friends. Marguerite "did not feel that it was strange that she had become a lesbian. Perhaps because it wasn't a topic when I was a child so I had no thought about it being dirty or bad."

She personalized the story of this friend by telling the group:

> I always keep people at a certain distance, both men and women. But also I think she was attracted to me. At the beginning I even denied that her being attracted to me had anything to do with sexuality. I liked her a lot but her girlfriend was very jealous. And when she told me the girlfriend was jealous I still was in denial of what this meant. I didn't really want to know and I felt afraid of sexual feelings.

She also described fleeing from men as intimacy approached. Later on, Marguerite spoke about commonalities and differences between lesbian and heterosexual feminists; the latter frequently want to include men in social events whereas the lesbians do not.

Yet Marguerite's relationships with women are extremely important to her: "I've always been very much in a female culture. My friends are basically women."

Marguerite concluded her comments in the group discussion by reiterating that she wants to develop her friendships and solidarity with women. To pursue relationships with men means possible unsatisfying involvement.

HILDE

Hilde's comments were intertwined with Marguerite's. She has one older brother and one younger sister. She believes there is a difference in the way sex is discussed in the United States and in Germany:

> The topic here is more hidden. In Germany we have it everywhere, you can see it on TV, on the late shows, on the magazines. . . . My feeling is that there is more discussion about it in public. We are still in the aftermath of the sexual revolution from the '60s and '70s in Germany. The topic is more widespread. But never talk about what you are doing. That is very hidden. Nobody talks about that.

Hilde also believes that women's roles in Germany are more sexualized. There is more "gawking" at women on the streets by men and nonsexual relationships with men are difficult to cultivate. Hilde's sense of self since coming to the United States has yielded more confidence in money matters, emotional expression, daily mobility, and a flexible work identity.

Her sexual self-awareness had not been profoundly impacted through immigration. As a young girl she was made aware of sex through explicit pornographic magazines she discovered in her brother's room. Magazines of this nature are widely available in Germany, and no shame is associated with buying them.

As a child she remembers seeing two men arm in arm in the street, and she was curious. Then as an adult, she had a gay male friend with whom she was perfectly comfortable. Neither male homosexuality nor lesbianism is problematic for her, "but this is not my way of living, that is not going to be my life."

Same-sex intimacy was neither discussed nor disparaged in her home growing up. Despite all the available information, Hilde feels that heterosexual communication is still lacking around sexual issues.

> [P]arents still talk about how important it is to be a virgin, but this was more for their generation, it is not so important for ours. Also it is difficult for women, even my feminist friends sometimes, to say what they want in bed. I know it was difficult for my mother to tell my father what she wanted.

Ironically, Hilde knows that her father

> would like to touch my mother more, to hug her and kiss her but she keeps him at a distance. My mother does not like to be touched, not even by the children . . . I understand that she does not want things to become sexual with my father, that she does not like sexuality, but I do not understand why she does not want to be touched by her children, although I guess it is all related.

Yet she understands her mother's unwillingness is due, in part, to her father's aggressiveness.

I can remember one of those evenings when he was yelling at
my mother and my mother started to yell at him. He did not
beat my mother, or at least very seldom, but this aggressive
behavior was very scary for all of us. Sometimes it made me
so sad as a child that I even wanted to commit suicide. But
my mother stayed with him because she did not want to be
alone with the children, at least he could support all of us.

Her sister repeated this pattern by marrying a violent man. But their
mother's injunction "to be very independent" has informed Hilde's
life's path.

She tried to teach me another way of living and to teach me
my rights even though she could not do it for herself. To be
independent from a man, and strong, and to earn my own
money. But we cannot talk to my father about this.

Hilde believes that her family background has affected her relationships. It makes her feel very afraid to hurt anyone by, for example, ending a relationship that she no longer desires.

Since coming to America, Hilde has deeply enjoyed the company
of only women friends:

for me it is very relaxing. I feel kind of tired of men, because
there is always the issue of the sexual interest. I only have one
male friend in America but he is over 60 years old, so there is
no problem.

In Germany every friendship with a man had the pressure to
become sexualized, so she disabused them of the possibility. Of the
results she said, "I was very sad to lose some male friends this way,
but I guess they were never really friends."

Through the narrative in English, Hilde, the least fluent of the
three, used a sprinkle of German words that either Ursula or
Marguerite translated. These little translations integrated into the
conversational flow and did not create interruptions in the process.
Overall, Hilde's experience in the United States has been "enjoyable
and subtly liberating."

URSULA

Ursula came to the United States in her late teens, prompted by her desire to escape from the influence of friends and an addiction to drugs and alcohol. She hoped it could be better controlled in the United States than in Germany. Indeed, the people she associated with in the United States did not use drugs; she freed herself from her addictions and started a new life in this country. In response to my initial question about early information on sex and sexuality, Ursula said

> I never talked about sexuality with my parents. Once when I was about 10 years old, my mother and I were on a beach and there was a couple making out. My mom very quickly, very nervously said, "You know, what happens between men and women. . . ." All the stuff I learned about sexuality was pretty much in school. In Biology we talked about sexuality, men and women sexuality.

Like Hilde, Ursula maintained an awareness of the possibility of violence by a man toward a woman after her father erupted at her mother when her mother had "caught" him with another woman.

Even though Ursula found more freedom in the United States to explore who she was, her sexual orientation was not the impetus behind her migration. She originally came as part of an Eastern religious community that, interestingly, helped her feel comfortable about her lesbianism.

> In that community I was very encouraged to experience my sexuality and whatever I felt in everything. It was completely okay for me to be lesbian or straight. . . . There were people there who had multiple partners and we were all encouraged to practice safe sex.

The tolerance of the community made her adjustment to the "regular world" difficult when she left it.

Ursula became sexual at age 20 despite exposure to sexual information a few years earlier. She commented on the cultural acceptance that affection between women in public enjoys in Germany. "You can, in Germany, see two women walk down the street arm in arm, hand in hand and it doesn't necessarily mean anything. It is accepted and respected to be affectionate." In the United States, this same behavior is labeled lesbianism. Ursula has been verbally insulted in America when showing affection toward a woman. Another difference is the availability of nude beaches in Germany where other nudists don't have sexual motives. Again, her experience in America contradicted this. Finally, in ideal bodily appearance, she also found the two cultures different: "I think there is more pressure on women here to follow the norm, to be a certain size, dressing a certain way. It is not so in Germany."

Describing the impact of migration on her life, Ursula believed the distance from her parents has let her

> come to my own about feeling pressure about conforming to what my parents want from me. Basically, they would still like to see me married and have kids. And still, sort of through "the back door" they always say that they hope I will turn straight.

Also she noted that self-reliance is culturally demanded in American society much more than in Europe.

> I feel very strongly I would have been a different person had I stayed in Germany, having had different influences. I would not be as strong, as self-confident. Having lived here, maybe having lived away from my family's security blanket, definitely has shaped me and has determined who I am now.

Ursula spoke at length about the topic of homosexuality and lesbianism. She detailed her life experiences and coming out. Homosexuality was a taboo topic, although she had an uncle who was gay and who came home to visit with his lover. She had been aware of male homosexuality but not lesbianism. Of lesbians, she thought, "they were really old and overweight, ugly, dangerous, old women."

Then she met a woman at school who gave her lesbian-related reading materials. As Ursula recalled:

> This was the first time I realized that I had a choice. That I could be with women and did not need to be with a man. I was

about 17 then and had severe crushes on teachers and friends but I never allowed myself to have any sexual experience then.

Her mother was unflinchingly accepting. Once they sat on a balcony, with the sun shining, and her mom looked at her and acknowledged her daughter's love of another woman. Ursula feels fortunate for her family's acceptance. Perhaps they sensed her innocence and accepted her because of it. "My parents never became angry with me. They just love me for who I am. So I never felt guilty about being homosexual." Ursula did feel guilty though, for her "unethical involvement" with someone who was in a relationship with another woman.

At this point, Ursula visibly hesitated, and then added, almost as if in a stream of consciousness:

> You know, I said earlier that I never regretted being a homosexual. Actually, over the last year I've wished many times that there was something that could turn us straight. The reason is the older I get the more I realize how difficult it is to live a gay lifestyle, how unaccepted it is, how much discrimination there is, how oppressive people are. It would just be easier because I am a very affectionate person and I love to be affectionate in public. Kiss, you know, hold hands, just live a regular life. And now that I am getting older I do care about what people think. I don't want people yelling at me and calling me names. That's why in the last year I have wished many times I were straight. Things would be so much easier. But I can't change who I am.

She pondered her lack of attraction to men, which makes even an attempt at heterosexuality impossible.

> But with a woman . . . I think every part of a woman is very attractive. So really, I would not be satisfied sexually if I were to live a straight lifestyle.

Toward the end of the group session, Ursula recalled a visit from her parents. Her father encouraged her to return to Europe to live in

Denmark and marry a woman. She understood this as his plea for proximity and also translated it as

> they respect me and accept me even though they would have wanted me to be straight. On the other hand they have not told anyone else in the family because they think it is nobody else's business. I know my mother blames my father because his brother is gay. She thinks it is in his family. Maybe she blames him for making me gay.

At the end of the group discussion I asked Marguerite, Hilde, and Ursula if they had felt comfortable talking in English. They said that it would have been easier to speak in German because they have better vocabulary in their native language. But all three—including Hilde who was the least fluent in English—said very emphatically that they did not know if they could have felt comfortable speaking in German about these topics. They said English allowed them to talk about these things without the embarrassment of German words that were forbidden from an early age.

Themes that emerged in this group session were often brought up by the 40 other respondents. The tone and depth of the conversations were much the same in all the other 40 cases. Because of this, other narratives will be presented in a more concise form. Lengthy quotes from other interviews will be provided only when some of the topics discussed are unique or when they address specific areas not previously discussed at length.

The three members of the second focus group were of Mexican origin. Despite the fact that Spanish was their native language, the discussion was conducted mostly in English. Once in a while some words in Spanish were mixed in the conversation. I made an effort to ask questions and make comments in Spanish, but Leticia, Angela, and Sandra reverted to English rather consistently.

LETICIA

Leticia grew up on the Mexican side of the U.S.-Mexico border. As a child she frequently crossed the border with her family to visit relatives in the San Ysidro–San Diego area. She moved permanently to the United States after her marriage to a Chicano (a U.S.-born Mexican American). She is now in her mid-40s and has two children, a 17-year-old son and a 12-year-old daughter.

During her childhood and adolescence, her mother never spoke to her about sex. Nor did her mother explain why her two brothers could do as they pleased while Leticia had to remain at home. Although the messages were unarticulated, Leticia felt penned in and always under surveillance. As an adolescent, she felt she must be "dirty" and "bad" since she needed so much surveillance. She understood that her mother's hypervigilance concerning her was sexually related and dominated by the fear of a possible pregnancy. Her mother frequently told her she would be "out of here" if she got pregnant, but never explained to Leticia how this could happen. When she became the mother of a daughter, she was determined not to behave like her mother. Thus she talks openly to her daughter about women's bodies and the importance of making her own decisions and avoiding shameful behavior. She also allows her daughter freedom to make decisions consonant with her age.

SANDRA

Sandra, who was 26 when she participated in the group, remembered her mother taking her to a female pediatrician when she was in the fourth or fifth grade. The pediatrician explained all she needed to know about menstruation. She thought then, "Is my mom so dumb that she cannot explain what all my classmates know?" To this day, there are major silences in her family about the body and sexuality.

Sandra's brother teases her, saying she knows nothing about sex because she is a virgin. She resents her brother's teasing, but prefers to keep silent to avoid trouble with her parents. Ironically, her mother pushes her to wear makeup and date but does not let her do so without a chaperone. Her parent's attitude toward her brother is completely different. He is told, "Go have sex if you want, just don't marry her"—precisely what they fear the men who date their daughter are told by their parents. But these contradictions are not verbalized in the family. At this point in the discussion, Sandra switched into Spanish to say, "I rather my parents and brother don't know what I know, so they don't think I am a 'dirty girl.'" Clearly, she hides her personal life from them to avoid conflicts.

ANGELA

Angela, who was fairly quiet during most of the discussion, spoke of her parents' age difference, which gives her father power over her mother beyond gender difference. Her father insisted that Angela and her slightly older sister date only with a chaperone. Recently, Angela has refused her father's dictum and sees her boyfriend unaccompanied. She asserted her independence from her father seven years earlier when she was diagnosed with cervical cancer. Her father had refused to allow his daughters to see a gynecologist because "those examinations could destroy their virginity." Prior to that she kept quiet and abided by his authority to avoid conflict; she feared that if she saw a gynecologist her family would think she was "bad," a judgment she apparently shared. When their family doctor referred her to a gynecologist for urgent care, her father readied to sue the doctor for intruding upon his daughter's body. When Angela realized her life was at risk, she stopped keeping quiet and started a new way of living.

Inge, Jazmin, and Sudha were members of the third focus group. Unlike the two previous ones, this group included women from diverse cultural and language backgrounds.

INGE

Inge, a German immigrant, was 45 at the time of the interview. She came to the United States at age 27 after marrying an American citizen in Europe. Her first years as an immigrant were confusing and difficult. She felt Americans were "puritanical" in matters of sex. Yet in other areas of social life she felt constricted by European norms of politeness that were less prevalent in America.

Inge's mother never spoke to her about sexual matters, though she vividly recalls her family's disapproval and disgust concerning homosexuality. Inge emphasized her attempts to educate her U.S.-born daughters to avoid her own mother's rigidities. Inge's comments did not challenge or add new information to the descriptions of German culture provided by Marguerite, Ursula, and Hilde.

A different perspective is provided by two other participants in this group: Jazmin, a serious and self-reflective Korean woman in her mid-thirties, and Sudha, a young Indian woman in her twenties.

JAZMIN

Jazmin arrived in the United States with her family in adolescence and later moved away from her parents to attend college. Jazmin found sex education in the United States cold and unromantic. Her mother's explanations about sex, "mumbled in Korean," also irritated her. Her mother believes no man is trustworthy, particularly Korean men. Jazmin has taken this advice seriously: She has never dated Korean men. Her mother, paradoxically, is disgusted by this. Jazmin's mother counsels her daughters against premarital sex and marriage to a White man. For this reason, Jazmin dares not introduce her White boyfriend to her parents. Jazmin believes that Koreans feel that a Korean woman who dates men outside her ethnic group is a "whore." Recently, when visiting some family friends, an old lady turned her back on her. This elderly woman accused Jazmin of shaming her mother by not yet marrying a Korean man when she is already of age to have several children.

Jazmin is also keenly aware of the racist sexual stereotype of Asian women who become intimate with non-Asians:

> Asian women are easily considered "whores" by outsiders when they are seen in public with White men. I worry about how I am perceived by strangers when I am affectionate in public with my Caucasian boyfriend. I know very well that my race is part of my attractiveness for some White men. I find it hard to believe that race is not always part of sexuality.

Although she loves her boyfriend, she believes their racial difference gives him additional power in the relationship in addition to the power he already has as a man.

Jazmin learned about sex in the United States. All of her relationships have been with White, American men. Thus, she acquired her vocabulary about sex in English. She thinks that she cannot use Korean words when talking about sex. Jazmin believes that growing up in the United States rather than Korea has made her more assertive and able to enjoy sex more than both Korean and White American women:

> Many Caucasian women, who are rather promiscuous in their sexual behavior, confess in private that they do not

enjoy sex. Korean women living in Korea, on the other hand, do not enjoy sex either and frequently feel "dirty" because of complying with their husbands' sexual demands.

I wonder whether Jazmin's gross generalizations about Asian and Caucasian women are not her own way of asserting her difference and uniqueness. During our conversation she spoke about her conscious effort at "fighting" the stereotype of the submissive Asian woman. She also spoke with pride about her mother's ability to fix cars and do a lot of things that are considered "a man's job."

SUDHA

Sudha, a young 23-year-old Indian woman, cannot imagine dating a non-Indian. In fact, she convinced her parents to forego an arranged marriage and allow her to date in college, because she has had only one boyfriend whose parents come from the same religion, social class, and region of India as hers. Sudha intends to have a career, unlike her silent, passive mother who has dedicated her life to a man. Yet she finds great pleasure in cooking for her boyfriend and taking care of him in what she denominates a "traditional way."

Sudha and her mother both dress in Western clothes, although her mother would much rather wear a sari. Sudha's father, however, forbids his wife wearing a sari; he believes them too sexually revealing for Western eyes. Another objection for him is that saris make his wife look "too traditional," which would contradict his professional status and his image as a "modern" Indian man. The irony of his "modern views" dictating his wife's attire seems to elude him.

Sudha feels a lot of compassion for her mother. Religion has been her mother's only support in Sudha's adjustment to life as an immigrant in the United States. Her mother's experience fuels her own determination to avoid an arranged marriage, yet she believes that arranged marriages are not necessarily bad.

Jazmin and Sudha are both more openly conflicted about loyalty to their families and cultural traditions than other study participants. They act "very American" yet express feelings of alienation in the midst of a racist society. In the group discussion they agreed it was difficult to acculturate to American society and argued that racism had played a major part in their distress. Jazmin and Sudha described being stereotyped by teachers and classmates during high school. But they acknowledge that living in the United States has offered economic opportunities for their families and greater choices for them as women.

MARIE-CLAIRE, SYLVIA, AND KERRINE

Three women born in the Caribbean islands have also been shaped by racism. Their stories share regional commonalities in both their initial experience of migration and in issues of sexual development.

Marie-Claire, Sylvia, and Kerrine migrated to the United States between the ages of 9 and 11 in the 1970s. Marie-Claire and Sylvia were born in Haiti and Jamaica, respectively, and Kerrine was born in England, shortly after her family migrated there from Jamaica. In her English childhood, Kerrine was surrounded mostly by White kids; hers was the only Black family in the neighborhood. For Sylvia and Marie-Claire, coming to the United States represented their first experience as "minorities." They had previously lived predominantly among people of color. All three reported difficulties adjusting to life in New York City, despite being surrounded by African Americans. Because these three women were "Black" by White American standards they gravitated toward Black Americans in New York. But racial similarity did not override cultural differences.

Marie-Claire, Sylvia, and Kerrine, now in their 30s, deeply identify with African Americans. In fact, they are "militant" and socially active on behalf of Americans of African descent. However, their sense of community and acceptance among African Americans was slow to evolve. Their hardest experiences as immigrant children came from cruel treatment by other children in the neighborhood and at school. Children picked fights with them, taunted and ridiculed them, and made life unpleasant in many ways. Their accents in particular were the source of ridicule and made them the target of unkind jokes.

Rejection from other Black children was a new and unwelcome experience for them all. They had expected racism and rejection from Whites but not from other Blacks, and this was painful. They describe the rejection they experienced and their coping with it as the most traumatic experience of their new lives. Interestingly, although Kerrine still preserves a strong British accent, neither Sylvia nor Marie-Claire have a trace of their foreign accents. Perhaps these childhood taunt-ings contributed to their "shedding" their geographic accents.

Teachers, on the other hand, were delighted with their distinct accents. They were frequently made to read aloud in class. This increased their embarrassment, and possibly the special attention fueled other children's jealousy. As newcomers, they in turn were shocked by the disrespectful tone used by American children to address their teachers and other adults in positions of authority.

Among many Caribbean families, it is common for mothers to leave their children behind with their own mother while they migrate and work to bring the family together at a later time. This was the case for both Kerrine and Sylvia. Kerrine's mother had left several children in Jamaica when she went to England. The older siblings rejoined the family years later when they relocated to the United States. Sylvia was left in Jamaica with her grandmother for several years. During this time she saw her mother only twice; her mother was "a picture on the night table." Then, when her mother sent for Sylvia and her brother, her grandmother refused to be left behind. They all came to the United States; grandmother continued her role as the children's care-taker, while Sylvia's mother's work supported them all. They initially encountered difficulty in bringing Sylvia's grandmother to the United States because of immigration policies. As Gabaccia (1994) has noted, "family reunification provisions fail to recognize the [family patterns] of many women in the Caribbean" (p. 62).

Marie-Claire's migration to the United States was problematized by her mother's death in Haiti just before her leaving. Her father had already immigrated to the United States some years before and had spent years trying to bring his family over. Before migrating, Marie-Claire lived with her mother, grandmother, several aunts, and their extended families, and did not really know her father. After her own mother's death the three children came to the United States to live with a father they barely knew. Marie-Claire found herself in an enclosed apartment in New York City without the companionship, support, or role modeling of the women in her mother's family. Her father "became both the father and mother" to her and encouraged her contact with Haitian women. When she first got her period, her father called a woman neighbor who spoke to her and told her what she needed to do.

The long-expected family reunions were far from idyllic. In Sylvia's case, her mother and grandmother fought frequently. Her grandmother disapproved of her daughter's life, and Sylvia's mother rejected her own mother's control after so many years of independence. Kerrine's siblings were rather angry with their mother for having left them behind. For Kerrine, the excitement of reuniting was tarnished by her older siblings' jealousy of the younger ones who had remained with their mother. Kerrine acquired two domineering older brothers who "watched her like hawks," a new and unpleasant experience for her. These familial conflicts were compounded by discomfort with American society and adjustments to life among their African American neighbors.

Although their societies of origin are not characterized by virulent misogyny, in Jamaica and Haiti gender determines a person's obligations and rights. This is frequently detrimental to women. All three families were extremely preoccupied with the dangers of their daughters' possible adolescent pregnancies. In fact, their mothers and grandmothers had become pregnant during adolescence. This parental injunction, initially annoying, served to spur them to pursue education. Parental disapproval of sexual activity deterred them from it until they were college age. Kerrine and Marie-Claire were both extremely naive and uninformed about sex, which also served to protect them. They both thought pregnancy occurred if they kissed a boy, and thus they were terrified of contact with boys until late in their high school years.

These three interviewees described adaptation to life in the United States as difficult and painful. All lost in social status and position as a result of the migration. The girls lost other "familiars" as well. Sylvia and Marie-Claire lost friends and relatives. All mourned the lack of open, green spaces. Marie-Claire in particular talks about this loss.

Interestingly, for Kerrine, the same Jamaican accent that cost her so much grief as a child is now, in adulthood, symbolic of "sexy men." She confesses to "falling for men" who speak with this accent even when she knows that the particular person may not be a good choice as a partner. Sylvia stays away from relationships with men of Jamaican descent, although she was not able to articulate the reasons for this conscious choice. Marie-Claire shows a marked preference for men who can speak Haitian Creole.

Sylvia is now a mother who finds herself telling her daughter what she herself was told: "Don't raise your skirt"; "Don't walk like that." It is odd to observe herself behaving "like Grandmother," yet it helps her develop an empathy for her mother and grandmother as she raises her daughter.

They all feel that gender made their migration experience different from their brothers'. Their families' preoccupation with their sexual behavior was a significant factor in their lives. Nevertheless, the three of them have seemingly achieved balance between their sexual interests and their professional lives.

MARITZA AND OLGA

Maritza and Olga are both Cuban; they migrated to the United States when they were 22 years old, during the 1970s. Olga comes from a middle-class family; Maritza comes from a poor working-class family. Maritza had come out as a lesbian in Cuba when she was 14. She had (and still has) considerable artistic talent as a musician and a poet. From a very early age she identified her lesbianism as a consequence of her artistic talent. (In Cuba and other Latin American countries there is a widespread association between artists and homosexuality that is widely accepted.) She was rebellious as an adolescent; she frequently came back home drunk in the middle of the night and more or less openly displayed her preference for girls. At the age of 22 she decided that because of the government's hostile position toward homosexuality, staying in Cuba was impossible for her. She was completely in favor of the Revolution and was politically supportive of it. She had connections in the government and was able to mastermind an escape during a trip to Eastern Europe sponsored by the Cuban government for young artists. Her family continues to live in Cuba. Even after all these years, they strongly disagree with her decision to leave the country. In the United States, Maritza refuses to participate in anything having to do with gay and lesbian activism and lives a very private life, although she makes no secret about her sexual orientation. Although she still writes poetry and composes music, she decided that "poems and songs were not going to feed her" and she actively pursued other professional endeavors. She quickly realized writing in Spanish did not provide her with a significant audience in an English-speaking country. Writing creatively in English was next to impossible for her. Both factors influenced her decision to enter another career. She is now a psychologist and has a fairly successful private practice. Her love relationships, with very few exceptions, have been with Spanish-speaking women. As I asked her quetions about language and sexuality she stated that she "cannot make love in English."

Unlike Maritza, Olga left Cuba because of her disagreement with the Revolution. She came to the United States with her family in one of the "freedom flights" instituted after 1968. She was aware of her feelings for other girls during her childhood and adolescence, but those feelings were never acknowledged then. She denied them because she was deeply Catholic and lesbianism was "sinful." She came out as a lesbian two years after arriving in the United States. She was still torn by the feeling that what she was doing was sinful. Despite those pangs of guilt, she was very much in love with another Cuban woman she had met in Los Angeles. They both began attending religious services at Dignity, a gay Catholic group then recently founded. Through Dignity, Olga became politically active in gay and lesbian issues within the lesbian community; this involvement continues to the present.

Olga is convinced that she would have never come out as a lesbian had she stayed in Cuba. In her view, the process of acculturation to U.S. society made it possible for her to come out. She has a master's degree in social work, works in a government agency, and services primarily Latinos. She remains mostly closeted in the Latino community for fear of the reaction the revelation of her lesbianism would elicit from clients and colleagues alike. However, she and her partner, a Jewish American woman, have decided to have a child. This has spurred her decision to come out to her colleagues.

LORENA

Lorena is a Puerto Rican–born nurse who emigrated to the U.S. mainland at age 30 and has been out as a lesbian for almost 20 years. Lorena learned about sex mostly from her school classmates. From an early age, Lorena understood that power and authority belonged to men:

> It is not that women were invisible. In fact, I grew up
> surrounded by women: my mother and my two grandmoth-
> ers, my father's five sisters, my many girl cousins. It's that it
> was very clear that men, not women, were "in charge." My
> father was the one who solved all his sisters' problems. When
> I was a child, I idealized and adored my father and grandfa-
> ther and was closer to my brother than to my sister. If I chose
> someone to emulate, it was my father, not my mother. I
> thought my father was very intelligent and always in
> command. Besides, I preferred balls to dolls. I was always
> more athletic, and playing outdoors. I had girlfriends but
> even with them I'd rather play ball.

Although Lorena's father had a strong and quick temper, male
violence never played a part in her thoughts about men and sex.

When Lorena grew up, she had to confront the realities of
women's lives and the idea of marriage. She found it hard to imagine
herself as a married woman, but had not considered the possibility of
lesbianism. During her college years, Lorena had male friends but
never imagined herself as a wife or a mother. Her sex fantasies then,
however, were all about men.

> It was hard to imagine that I could be married, but I had not
> given a serious thought to any alternatives. So I thought I
> would marry an ex-priest: He would probably be more intel-
> lectual, not as "macho," and possibly be an American. . . . I
> think this idea was coupled with the realization that since I
> could not be a priest I could perhaps be a nun. But instead,
> rather than being a nun or marrying a priest, I fell in love
> with a nun.

A general sense of dissatisfaction with her everyday life in Puerto
Rico prompted her emigration to the mainland United States. Like
all Puerto Ricans, she was an American citizen: No major legal
preparations were required. She hoped that a change in the environment and autonomy from her family would energize her life, and
didn't foresee what this change would entail. Shortly after her arrival
in the United States, Lorena met a longtime lesbian and fell in love

with her. A quick transformation occurred. In her words, "it was as if the pieces of a puzzle had now all suddenly fit in place." She had been "out" as a lesbian for almost 20 years at the time of the interview. Since coming out, she has only returned to Puerto Rico for brief visits.

She speaks with some degree of comfort about her sexual orientation—in the United States and in English. She is far less comfortable speaking of it in Spanish or in Puerto Rico. She attributes this to the plethora of "dirty words" in Spanish that describe lesbians, and also to her family's presence in Puerto Rico.

> I can be out in English but not in Spanish. When the plane lands in Puerto Rico it is as if I "shut down" and do not become a lesbian again until I come back to the U.S. It took me forever to say certain words in English. It is still impossible to say those words in Spanish. I can now find pride in saying some words in English but I still feel only shame saying those words in Spanish. I would only use those words when absolutely necessary to talk to a Latina lesbian, not on my own. . . . It is not that I think that English is "liberating" or that people are so "free" in this country. It is just that lesbianism is more visible here . . . and, besides, English is much less charged for me, not only about sexuality but about practically anything emotional.

When I asked which language she preferred while making love, she said she uses both languages but that English "comes easier" because she discovered her "lesbian self" in English. She is fluently bilingual but believes that some parts of her emotional self are more "in English" while others are more "in Spanish."

She equates her lesbianism to another form of biculturalism: "You are always on the margins. Being gay or lesbian is living in a different subculture. Being a Latina immigrant is like that too." Despite her sense of marginality, she believes her coming out was eased by being in the United States. She explained that "There is only one organized group in Puerto Rico that produces a publication in Spanish about gay and lesbian life—*Sal pa' fuera*." She discovered this group in a recent visit to Puerto Rico. It was rather surprising to know that even this existed. "But, of course, I have lived away from Puerto Rico for the last 20 years and changes do occur."

Lorena visits her parents at least once a year, frequently accompanied by a woman lover. She made love in her parents' house for the first time two years ago; prior to that, it felt like forbidden territory for lovemaking. She continues to perceive her family and Puerto Rican culture as inhibitors of her sexuality. Although there are now gay discotheques in Puerto Rico, Lorena has never visited any of them.

She believes that the life stage at which her migration occurred made a difference. The shifts in identity necessitated by the coming out process, which followed shortly after her migration, contributed to her already solid personal identity. Although it was initially "foreign" to see herself as a lesbian, being a lesbian "felt right," and she did not have doubts about "who she was."

CINDY

Cindy, a native Taiwanese, came to this country when she was 2 years old. She remembers little about her native land. Due to her age at migration, she never learned of sex or a sexual vocabulary in Chinese. Her knowledge of Chinese comes from her parents, who never spoke about sex, let alone lesbianism. Her parents always spoke to her in Chinese, and she was teased by her Chinese American schoolmates whenever they overheard her use her native tongue.

Cindy remembered being affectionate toward another seventh-grade girl and their schoolmates' taunts that they were "homos." Unaware of the term's meaning, she intuited it as pejorative. She asked her older brother, who reassured her that the term referred to "homo sapiens," which meant human being and therefore lacked all negative implications. Years later, after coming out, Cindy was amused at her and her brother's limited knowledge of English slang terms concerning sexuality at the time. Despite this youthful crush, she willingly pursued heterosexual relationships as an adult.

Cindy's mother told her about menstruation but never connected it with sex. In fact, her mother said very little about men and sex: "Do not be 'cheap,' do not get pregnant, marry only Chinese." Cindy conversed with other girls about getting pregnant. In one such talk, schoolmates told the story of a girl who had gotten pregnant "because she cared too much about her football-player boyfriend." Cindy internalized this to mean it was better not to "care too much" about any boy just in case she could get pregnant without knowing why. Now she also remembers this story with amusement as another episode that showed her naivete in these matters.

During her college years, Cindy was sexually involved with a White man she loved deeply. Neither set of parents were happy with this relationship, and all tried to end their involvement. Eventually, the man broke off the engagement, unable to tolerate the pressure. When the relationship ended, Cindy was devastated. She relied on her friendship with a female college classmate to support her through these bad times; eventually, they became lovers.

She has lived as a lesbian since then; Cindy is now in her mid-40s. For her, her lesbianism was just one more thing she could not share with her rigidly traditional parents. She was unable to talk to them about anything that mattered to her, so keeping her lesbianism a secret was not that difficult.

Language informs Cindy's sexuality in interesting ways. Since she spoke Chinese only with her parents, she has never spoken about her sexuality in Chinese. None of her sexual partners have been Chinese, so she has not had the opportunity to speak about sexuality in an intimate context either. She is close friends with a Chinese gay man, but they do not address sexual issues. Their discussions focus on restrictions and prejudices against gays and lesbians in Chinese culture and families.

Cindy believes that immigration has affected her far less than her immigrant family has. She believes immigration made her parents more restrictive and conservative than they would have been had they stayed in Taiwan. She now lives as far away as possible from her parents because even at her age, she feels constricted by their rigidity. Nevertheless, she is out to them and, even though they do not talk about it or approve, they have not rejected her. Interestingly, she also believes that had she not felt so restricted by her parents she might not have become a lesbian:

> To be a lesbian is another way of rebelling against them. Had my family stayed in Taiwan, they may not have felt the need to be so controlling and I may not have felt the need of

rebelling by being a lesbian. In fact, I may have just married. After all, I was ready to marry my college boyfriend. If they would have been less restrictive, I would have been less rebellious. That is why I say it is not the culture, it is my parents' migration that made a difference. I became a lesbian not because it was appealing to me or because it was "cool" but because it was one more of the things they did not approve of. They helped destroy my most important love relationship.

Cindy's anger toward her parents may still be very present in her life choices. She left college when the love relationship with her White boyfriend dissolved, and as another rebellion she shunned graduate school.

After the traumatic ending of her heterosexual love affair, "the attraction to a woman felt very familiar"—very much like the intense same-sex friendship she had had in seventh grade. Although she did not consider herself a lesbian in this early relationship and just described it then as "being very good friends," she is now completely out and is one of the leaders in the Asian American lesbian community. In retrospect, she compares her early denial of lesbianism to her denial of being Chinese while in her mixed-race heterosexual relationship.

AURELIA

Aurelia, a 31-year-old lesbian, has an Australian mother and a Thai father. Her family moved frequently during her youth: Australia, Thailand, and the United States. She identified two ethnic identities: one Australian, the second Thai. During her childhood, she wanted to be solely Australian, "because I was a snob and believed that Thai culture was inferior." Then, in adolescence, her family moved to Thailand where she met "a British man who was more of a snob than me." This became a turning point that prompted her reclamation of her Thai identity. Ten years ago, her family moved to the United States. Now she feels mostly American but continues to visit family in Thailand and Australia. She identifies with both these cultures. Coming out as a lesbian added another dimension to her multicultural identity. Aurelia reflects that

As a lesbian, I am an American. This is where I came to this identity and where I learned the meaning of lesbianism. I didn't know anything about Thai lesbian culture. But the Thai view of sexuality still influences me deeply.

Of particular importance is the contrast between the Buddhist and Western beliefs in fate and choice:

The Buddhist culture of Thailand assumes a certain Karmic influence on all sexuality, rather than seeing it as a choice like Westerners do, with its implication that it can be the wrong choice.

Although Thais do not talk much about sexuality, they do not reject their gay children. Sons who may be "drag queens" are still in charge of the family's business despite some family embarrassment about them.

Aurelia's self-doubts about being a lesbian come from her mother's Western perspective:

My mother is a behaviorist at heart. She is always concerned about the influence of the environment, so she always worries about what made this child lesbian.

Her father, by contrast, took the Buddhist perspective and accepted her lesbianism very quickly.

Aurelia determined earlier in her life not to act like the stereo-typically submissive Asian woman. The influences of her Thai grand-mother and aunts were balanced by her mother's progressive perspectives and Aurelia's Western education. "The interesting thing is that my aunts are mild mannered in public but really abrasive at home."

Aurelia's mother never addressed any sexual matters with her, including menstruation. But when Aurelia visited Thailand after menarche, her female relatives talked about it aloud among them-selves. This she found "embarrassing but good."

Even though Aurelia's mother shuns sexual discussions, she

frequently broaches Aurelia's sexual identity and insists that she "should give heterosexuality a chance."

In Thailand the English words "gay" and "lesbian" are the ones used because there are no Thai words for these sexual identities; words exist only for men or women who cross-dress. The Thai language has words for generational distinctions but not for gender ones. Aurelia remembered with a mixture of pride and amusement that her aunt asked her once

> if any of my girlfriends had boyfriends and then added, "or are you each other's boyfriends?" Because the word for "boyfriend" and "girlfriend" is gender-neutral in Thai, she could say that without problem. She obviously knows [I am a lesbian] and has never asked me if I'll marry a guy.

Aurelia recalled,

> Thais usually assume that boys and girls explore same-sex relationships because it is forbidden to have encounters with the opposite sex. Because of this belief, adolescents of the same sex can be all over each other: hold hands, touch. This happens always, but particularly in adolescence. It is very rare to see men and women affectionate in public with each other and much more common to see the same sex all over each other. . . . But this is not necessarily a sexual gesture.

Western languages, according to Aurelia, have more words for romance and feelings, but Thais are better at expressing the feeling.

A relationship with a Thai woman went most smoothly when they spoke only Thai. In Thai, Aurelia felt freer to speak affectionately and so did the other woman. She "felt like this person could do me no harm in Thai."

For Aurelia, Thai is a second language: She grew up speaking English in Australia, and her mother speaks no Thai. Thus, her choice of language follows the same pattern of most of the others interviewed: preference for the second language—Thai in her case—in the context of sexuality and relationships.

EVA

From a very early age, Eva's life has been full of changes and migrations. In the course of all these moves, Eva learned several languages. She is now fluent in German, English, and French and can converse with relative ease in several other languages. She was born in Vienna in an upper-class Jewish family. Her ancestors were early Zionists who promptly left Austria after Hitler's 1938 *Anschluss* and returned there at the end of World War II. It was then that her parents married and she was born. Her father's business took the family to other European countries as well as to South America and Asia during Eva's childhood. The family returned to Austria, where her parents still live, during Eva's late adolescence. Then, at the age of 20, she migrated on her own to the United States, ostensibly to study. She had no real intentions to return to Austria.

Eva reminisced,

> I thought of the United States as Disneyland. It was wonderful. I was frantically bored as a child, there were very few books in the school libraries, few children with whom to speak in any language. . . . In the U.S. there were so many TV programs, so many toys. . . . I loved Barbie dolls as a child and Barbie was American. . . . I can't remember anything negative in the U.S. It was always a wonderful and stimulating country. I felt free. I felt there were unlimited opportunities here to read and talk to people.

Eva's mother, a very distant person, made Eva feel "peripheral to her life":

> it was my father who told me that girls should be virgins until they married and who would buy Kotex for me because my mother never seemed to be around. [However,] my mother was the one who told me about menstruation and about heterosexual intercourse. She said, "the way it happens is a man lies on top of a woman and a drop passes between them and they have a baby." That sounded rather confusing to me. A drop of what? I don't know if she ever told me anything about being a woman but she was so strikingly beautiful that

I knew I could not be attractive. I was a plump child, which was a huge issue in my family. In fact, I had no choice but to be a tomboy. Instead, I focused on being a smart child. . . . I was almost raised as my father's son because I was an only child.

Eva received encouragement for her intellectual pursuits from her father. He also stressed that she should marry a Jewish man. He told her repeatedly that she would never marry if she continued to be overweight. Later in life, she feared no woman would like her because of her weight. But as an adolescent, she found relief in the knowledge that she should wait for sex until she was married, because

I was very attracted to girls since I was 4, so the idea of having sex with boys was horrifying. In fact, there were no Jewish boys anywhere in any of the countries we lived in, so that made me feel very safe.

Eva's governess, like her father, also pressured her toward a heterosexual union. She wanted her to be married and frequently talked about her future wedding. In response, Eva said, "I spent a lot of my life telling her and others that I would never get married so I think my family got used to hearing it."

Eva had far more opportunities to be with girls than boys, because she always went to single-sex schools. She had intense friendships with girls and at a very early age realized these entailed sexual feelings. During adolescence she was closeted because of peer pressures. She invented crushes with movie stars or an unavailable boy to have an acceptable pretext to initiate conversation with a girl in her class with whom she was "madly in love." When Eva turned 16, this girl gave her a very expensive gold ring as a proof of their friendship. This did not arouse suspicion since intense same-sex friendships were encouraged for adolescents in Austria.

When Eva talked about her adolescent sexual feelings and ideas, she did so mostly in English. At that time she was attending the American International School in Vienna, and she associated English with sex even though her classmates' first language was German like hers.

Eva began having sexual relationships only after she came to the

United States and most of her partners have spoken English. Only once did she have a relationship with another native German speaker.

> I loved that we could speak German to each other. It was the first time I learned some of the words for lesbian culture, lesbian sex, in German.

Occasionally Eva returns to Austria. When she visits her friends there she has

> this feeling of "there but for the grace of God, go I" because I would have been like them if I had stayed in Austria. I was very much of a good girl and I probably could have married a man. I certainly cannot imagine finding a lesbian culture in Austria.

Eva is very much aware of her competing identities:

> [I am] very hard to categorize because I can tell my story as a lesbian, as a Jewish woman daughter of Holocaust survivors, as an immigrant, as an overweight woman, and of course, as a White, European, upper class woman. So I have different stories depending on the context.

MAYA

Maya, also born in Europe (the Netherlands), has also lived in several countries. Unlike Eva's case, the reasons for Maya's multiple migrations were completely personal; her family continues to live in her country of birth. She came to live in the United States almost by chance. In the late 1970s she came to visit some friends and met a woman with whom she fell in love. They have been a couple since then.

Maya feels very strongly about her Jewish identity. World War II was a defining event for her life because it completely altered her parents' lives. She firmly believes in the intergenerational transmission of trauma. The war is emotionally present for her despite the fact that she was not born until its end. Her identity has been primarily defined by her Jewishness and the Holocaust; being a lesbian is secondary for Maya. This is likely because for her family and in Holland, being a lesbian is not problematic. Maya thinks Americans are puritanical and create "unnecessary fuss about these things."

Despite her comfort with lesbian sexuality, for her, "lesbianism is more of an emotional orientation rather than a sexual orientation."

Her use of language reveals her multiple identifications. She feels comfortable swearing in English but cannot bring herself to say the equivalent words in Dutch. If she were to do so they would have more emotional meaning. Sometimes it is easier to explain some things in English "because some important parts of my identity developed in English."

CECILIA

Cecilia, a 60-year-old successful classical concert pianist, left Puerto Rico when she was 16 to attend college in the United States. She sought permanent relocation because she found Puerto Rico "an intolerably sexist country." From watching American movies and reading magazines, she erroneously believed that the United States was free of sexism. Since then, her experiences here have shown her otherwise.

Several years before she left Puerto Rico, Cecilia's mother taught her about menstruation and "how babies are made." She was cautioned about men and chaperoned at dances. These precautions seemed contradictory to her, since her older brother had repeatedly sexually molested her at home and no one seemed to notice. Her father's womanizing caused much fighting between her parents, which she overheard. Her father's and brother's behaviors combined with the warnings and precautions made her fearful of men.

Both in Puerto Rico and during college in the United States, Cecilia dated young men and engaged in "some kissing and petting." Soon after her arrival, she developed a crush on another girl and they started kissing and touching. When Cecilia went to Puerto Rico for Christmas vacation, they exchanged long, intense love letters. Her mother found one of these letters and her parents decided she could not return to the United States. She convinced her parents to send her back, this time to a strict Catholic college, and promised abstention from lesbianism. She finished college and eventually married a White, American, Catholic man.

The marriage, which was her only heterosexual relationship, lasted for more than 20 years. During it she was completely monogamous, until after 23 years of marriage (and two children), both husband and wife had affairs with women. Cecilia requested a divorce and went to live with her woman lover. Since then, more than 20 years ago, Cecilia has lived as a lesbian.

All of Cecilia's female partners have been Jewish. None have spoken fluent Spanish. It is more comfortable for her to speak in English when discussing sex because none of her partners have been Spanish speakers, and because she learned about sex in the United States. During the interview, she always used English when referring to her sexual experiences. Her last two partners spoke a little Spanish and specifically asked her for some sensual or loving verbal expressions they could use during sexual encounters. Referring to her present partner, she said that

> whenever she uses words or expressions in Spanish, it touches me deeply; the intensity increases. Spanish carries a lot of feeling. But it also carries shame. Sex words in Spanish are dirty; talking about parts of the body in Spanish feels shameful. It is like I have Spanish encapsulated in some part of me; I have "put away" words and feelings in Spanish. But because Spanish carries all this feeling, it is liberating to use Spanish; it is like a sexual eye-opener to use Spanish but it also gives me an insight on how much shame I carry in Spanish.

In this statement, Cecilia articulated clearly what other interviewees implied in discussing their use of language around sexual issues.

Cecilia is out to her entire family: parents, siblings, aunts, uncles, children, and some grandchildren. All have responded with silence. Like Cindy, Cecilia feels "cut off inside" from her family. Lesbianism is just one more thing that "cuts her off" from them. It did not cause the distance.

For these women, migration offered freedom and freer lesbian lives. Their political, religious, and social affiliations with the lesbian community varied greatly. But they share the link between migration and sexual self-expression. Maritza and Olga are out to their families

after initial reluctance; others, like Aurelia and Maya, find no particular conflict with family members over their lesbianism. Eva's family
conflicts had more to do with her weight than her lesbianism. Lorena
and Cindy have found it more difficult to come out to their families
despite their political involvements in the lesbian community.

Cecilia has lived away from her family of birth most of her life. For
her the freedom to live a lesbian life came many years after her immigration but nonetheless was contingent upon the distance.

SHELO

Like many young Tibetans, Shelo was born in India. Her family
escaped to India after the Chinese invaded Tibet. She was considered
a citizen of Nepal when she decided to migrate to the United States.
Her family was poor, and this necessitated her working to earn a
living at the age of 11. She has been in the United States since the
age of 18 and was 26 at the time of interviewing. A resourceful and
energetic young woman, Shelo immigrated with the assistance of a
cousin living in France. She describes herself as

> a "village girl" who knew very little about anything. My
> cousin came to visit and told us very good things about
> "Inji"—Tibetans call "Inji" all the places and people who are
> foreign, meaning Europeans or Americans and their coun-
> tries—so he talked about "Inji" and said good things and my
> mother asked me if I wanted to go to "Inji." In Tibet women
> do not ask too many questions. So I said yes and he took me
> to the French embassy and paid the money. I went to France
> for one month and a half. There I got a visa for the U.S. for
> six months. In the U.S. I stayed with friends of my cousin in a
> rural area in California. My greatest surprise when I saw these
> "Inji" places was that there were trees and plants and flowers.
> I had always thought that in "Inji" there were only concrete
> buildings and cars . . . you can see how ignorant I was.

Her language abilities and yearning for Tibet were significant
obstacles for her: "I needed to find work but I did not speak any
English and was very homesick. I watched television all day. I was
disappointed."

As she established community, her prospects and spirits improved:

> I went to live in Berkeley with three Tibetan girls. They
> came to meet me at the BART station and it was like a bless-
> ing thread started. At first I knew only 5 people in this area,
> now I know about 120. They found me a job as a live-in
> babysitter: $150 a week, six days a week from 7:00 a.m. to
> 10:00 p. m. I learned English from the kids.

But her homesickness continued. She was conscious of the need to
legalize her status through a job that would yield a green card. She
hoped an American citizen in the Buddhist Center might help her, but
discovered "Inji" men's sexual motives instead. She eschewed their
advances and bestowed her nonsexual attention on a Tibetan man
with whom she moved to Los Angeles. "He had me convinced that he
was a reincarnated Lama and I was lucky that he had chosen me."
    The illusion of their platonic bond shattered when this man had
sex with her without her consent.

> It was not my will. I was proud of being a virgin. All I remem-
> ber is that it hurt and that I missed my mom. It was like a big
> part of me fell. I felt small and like something was lost. But
> then, this was my karma. Now this was my husband.

Disillusioned by the countryman whom she had trusted, she was
further hustled by an attorney—an Indian man—who promised to
help her. Her "husband" exploited her financially—indeed stole her
earnings—while promising the coveted green card.
    She tried to make this relationship work for one year:

> I had grown up in a culture that said that women should
> tolerate what their husbands did. I should be thankful for my
> karma rather than complain about it.

But then, two unexpected events gave her the courage and the
opportunity to move out of this relationship. She became pregnant
and her "husband" fell in love with another woman. She had an abor-

tion and moved out, relieved of the relationship. Yet her economic prospects were still grim:

> I stayed with a friend who got me a job. Another live-in job . . . workers are slaves, you know. They paid me $800 after working for three months. I used to cry and feel sorry for myself.

But she would not be discouraged. She returned to the Bay area, extended her work permit, and pursued school part-time as a nurse's aide. At the time of the interview, she was employed in a hospital. She now has her green card. Her personal life has also become much better. She married an American who helped her secure her green card. This restored her faith that "not all 'Injis' are bad after all." The couple visited India, where Shelo's mother approved of their union.

Shelo learned little about sex from her mother, who had only "spoken about" menstruation. A substantial portion of her sexual knowledge came from her two marriages. She feels she has "broken out of her culture" because of her experiences. The two closest people to her are her husband and a Jewish American woman who is her teacher; neither of them is Tibetan. In concluding, Shelo said:

> I am very happy I came. However, I am not a real American and I am not a real Tibetan. I don't fit in Tibetan society anymore. I don't know what is the secret about all this. . .

MEI

Political events also caused Mei's migration. Her family has emigrated twice: first to Taiwan from mainland China, escaping the Chinese revolution, and later, from Taiwan to the United States in the late 1950s where she has lived since then. Mei's family was upper-class nobility in China. At times this has created difficulties in Mei's relationships with other Chinese women, since they feel intimidated by her family background. Only once, while she was in college, did she date a Chinese American man. She married a European American man. She attributes her choice to the authoritarian attitudes of Chinese men. Her parents expressed disapproval about her choice of spouse, but Mei reminded them that her own brother was domineering and abusive toward his wife. She told them she would not be involved with a man like her brother. In her eyes, he typifies the behavior of most Chinese men.

During her childhood in Taiwan, Mei was aware of her class status. Her mother and grandmother prohibited her and her siblings from mixing with other Taiwanese children and from speaking in Taiwanese dialect.

Their high social status changed abruptly when she came to the United States. Here she was seen as just another Chinese girl by both Anglos and Chinese Americans. Initially she had difficulties in school because she knew no English upon her arrival. Her poor performance contributed to her sense of humiliation and confusion; in Taiwan she had always been an excellent student—indeed, in a year and a half in the United States she had mastered the language and moved to the head of the class.

Because they were accustomed to respect from other Chinese and were no longer recipients of it, immigration created great stress for her family. Also, Mei and her siblings had to adjust to living in a two-parent household again: Her father had come to the United States several years ahead of his family, so they had been living separately. This was a difficult adjustment for her mother, too. She had been the head of the household, sharing authority and receiving support from her own mother; now she had to adjust to her husband's authority and her mother's absence.

During adolescence, Mei's knowledge of gender roles came from her mother's prohibitions. Her mother advocated traditional behaviors more than her father and never spoke of sex. (Even now, though Mei is middle-aged, they never mention this topic.) Mei learned about anatomical sexual issues in sex education classes. She was not scared when she began menstruating, because her older sister had talked to her about her own experience and shown her a sanitary napkin.

Mei associates sexual arousal with English because she is married to a man who does not speak Chinese. All their sexual interactions are in English. Mei believes that she is more comfortable with sex than most White American women she knows, for several reasons. She believes that Judeo-Christian religious taboos hinder women's sexual pleasures. She is not affected by that religious background, nor did she live in China or Taiwan long enough to be influenced by those cultural sexual taboos.

Given her youth when she left China and Taiwan, she acquired her "sex vocabulary" in English. She knows no sexual words in Chinese, although she learned some swearing and "dirty" words in Taiwanese.

In daily conversations with family members and other Chinese-speaking individuals, she mixes English and Chinese. Mei believes that schooling in English "changed her head." She feels that she does not belong anywhere because she has been a refugee twice and feels perpetually a transient. This has affected her attitude in relationships. Even though she has been married for fifteen years, she feels she is "always a little too ready to leave relationships."

LIN

Lin is also Chinese. She was born in Taiwan, where her family sought refuge after the Chinese revolution. Her parents migrated to the United States because they believed their children's education would be limited in Taiwan. Both her parents spoke English before coming to the United States, but Lin did not. In school, she learned rapidly and found English easier to learn than Chinese.

The move away from her family to attend college was more dramatic than the transition between Taiwan and the United States (I can speculate that the transition to college reactivated half-conscious losses she experienced leaving Taiwan). In college, Lin took classes in Mandarin Chinese; she wanted to learn the language of her ancestors. This choice speaks to her need to recover losses from her migration, reactivated when she left home for college. Lin returned to Taiwan during her college years, seeking redefinition and clarification of her identity as either Chinese or American. But she

> hated it. I thought it was dirty, hot, crowded. I did not like the people or the environment. It was a terrible disappointment. Besides they thought I spoke Chinese with an American accent, so I was not really Chinese.

Also while in college, Lin was "caught in the epidemic of eating disorders that was prevalent there." For two years she vomited regularly after lunch to maintain her weight. Although she had read the classic self-help book *Our Bodies, Ourselves*, she "was rather ignorant about my body until college." She never confided in her parents about her eating disorder or about sex. During recovery from the eating disorder she got in touch with her body. At this time, she met the man who eventually became her husband; he is European American. She was concerned her parents might reject him, but they were very open. His race has never been an issue. In fact, the day she graduated from college he took her to a fancy hotel to spend the night; the next morning she called her mother and before Lin could say anything, her mother said, "My little girl has grown up!" Through her husband, Lin learned a lot about sex. That may be why her sex vocabulary is in English. Interestingly, her mother uses her "broken English" rather than Chinese whenever she wants to discuss emotional topics.

Lin, a committed feminist, is very involved in political activities. Her mother influenced her favorably in this respect. Though her mother comes from a traditional family, she does her own work and created an egalitarian marriage. Lin is very conscious of "fighting the stereotype of passive Asian women." She and her husband see themselves as "political agents, fighting traditional constructions of masculinity and femininity." She realizes that being with a White man "protects her from some of the consequences of racial oppression." While her family is certainly not a "typical Chinese family," Lin believes that they are more "traditional than the average American family." Her relationship with her husband, she thinks, has taught her to see herself differently from "the typical Chinese perspective on women." This has helped her to be freer sexually and otherwise.

NORIKO

Noriko also believes she is not the "typical" Asian woman. Noriko is a 33-year-old unmarried Japanese woman. She came to the United States to get a college degree and decided to stay.

When Noriko turned 20, her family planned to give her a ceremonial kimono, which entails a great expense. Noriko told her parents, "no kimono; send me to America," and they agreed.

In her trips to the United States and her decision to stay, Noriko has been supported by her stepmother, the only mother Noriko knew. Her parents divorced when she was seven years old and she has not seen or heard from her biological mother since. Her father married soon thereafter, to a professional woman who

> demanded to go to college in Japan when less than half of all girls were finishing high school. Because she is so intent on the education of women, she pushed me through high school. In fact, I remember once she was furious with me because I was wearing makeup. She thought that meant I was going to become a frivolous girl who would not want to study. She was both good and bad for me because she pushed so much.

Her stepmother's gender consciousness profoundly impacted Noriko's life course. With her help, Noriko spent a summer with some family friends living in the Midwest. The next year, she found another opportunity to come, this time for a year. She returned to Japan again and applied to American graduate school. When she was admitted, her parents allowed her to go with the stipulation that she return to Japan after her schooling was complete. Noriko agreed, and at that time had honestly intended to do so. But when she completed her master's degree, she took a job with a Japanese American company that obtained a green card for her. She accepted the job, and describes her position as "half translation, half being a cultural bridge."

Noriko feels she has changed a lot since relocating to the United States. She does not know if the changes are due to migration or to simply aging. However, she does feel a greater degree of freedom in America to do what she wants than she did in Japan.

Her language usage repeats a now familiar theme. In general it is easier for her to use Japanese than English. However,

> certain things I cannot explain in Japanese and are better said in English. For example, "I love you" is not completely equivalent to what you say in Japanese translation. I mean it is "heavier" if you say these things in Japanese. "I like you," "I love you," "I care about you," I don't know if you can say all these things completely in Japanese. When we say, "I love

you" it is really committed. But here sometimes Japanese women say "I love you" too much because it is easier to say in English.

Noriko also referenced different styles of clothes worn by professional women in Japan and the United States. In Japan, she noted, women dress "more feminine."

The longer she lives in the United States the more distant and "different" she feels from other women living in Japan.

> As a professional woman I don't fully fit in in Japan. I feel smothered. Unable to be myself. On the other hand, American women are not as free as they say in Japan. When you live here you see battered women, discrimination in the workplace, women are violated. You understand the stories about liberation and about sex are not true and that women are not equal. But I think here people are more aware. In Japan, despite difficulties, women are also coming to their own. But I feel more freedom here. I can be myself.

Noriko spoke of her comfort being a woman and in women's company. In fact, she prefers groups of women to mixed company. At this point she hesitantly said,

> I don't know. I am not sure if this is coming from losing my own mother. Maybe there is a longing in my heart. Because of my childhood path . . . because all of a sudden my mother was gone. But there is a feeling in my heart. I'm not saying I'm gay, but it seems I notice beauty in women more than I notice how good-looking a guy is. People say all women get that but I'm not sure. Maybe I am unconsciously thinking of my mother . . . you know it is somewhere in my mind. I talk better with women.

The loss of her biological mother at such an early age has deeply affected Noriko. In the interview's most emotional moment, Noriko described a woman in Los Angeles who reminded her vividly of her mother. Noriko was paralyzed, and could not say a word. Her friend told this woman, "You look like her mother." The two looked at each other for a long moment but did not say anything. Noriko apologized to the unknown woman for her confusion, and she left. But she believes one day she will meet her mother again; on that day she will know it is her mother.

SISSY

Sissy, a 23-year-old Korean woman, spoke extensively about the influence of her mother's behavior on her. Sissy came to the United States when she was 4 years old and has lived here since then. Her parents divorced during Sissy's adolescence. She attributes their decision to the influence of American culture on them. In the Korean community this was a source of embarrassment for her. Sissy knows that the divorce was precipitated by her father's behavior. He was public about having a mistress, another Korean woman. Yet despite his culpability, Sissy wished her mother had not divorced him; no other relative had ever divorced. She remains afraid of her strict father but loves and respects her mother. Her mother has sacrificed significantly for her children despite the divorce's financial and emotional difficulties.

Not surprisingly, Sissy mistrusts men. She is still a virgin and plans to remain so until marriage. Her only knowledge of sex comes from instruction given through the church. She recounted with amusement that she took "the birds and the bees" story to be literally true without grasping its real meaning. She can not picture her mother ever speaking about sex. However, her older sister is "very promiscuous." More than once she has heard her mother fighting with this sister about the latter's behavior.

At the university in Korea, Sissy's mother was the only woman in her class. Sissy's pride in this prompted her decision to study hard to please her mother. She is an excellent student. Despite Sissy's successes, her mother regrets not having a son. Her regret that she is son-less, coupled with her divorce, makes her mother feel a failure. This compromises Sissy's self-worth: No matter how hard she tries she is not enough for her mother.

Sissy is losing her Korean language skills because she migrated at such an early age. Although they still speak it at home, her vocabulary in Korean does not keep pace with her use and knowledge of English.

Since Sissy speaks hardly at all about sex, language preference when doing so is a non-issue.

MANEL

Manel, unlike Sissy, is rather proud of her sexual experience. She attributes this comfort to two factors: Women in her family have had power for many generations, and her family's many migrations have required constant adaptations to the unknown.

Manel is from Sri Lanka. Her parents, both scientists, came to study in the United States when she was a baby. They moved to Nairobi after receiving their doctorates; she grew up in Africa. At the time of the interview, Manel had lived in the United States for five years and intended to stay. She recently returned to Sri Lanka, visited her extended family, and went to Kenya, where her parents still live. After these trips, she decided that despite her comfort in both "countries of her youth" she would stay in the United States.

Manel's recent two months' visit with her grandmother and aunts in Sri Lanka confirmed for her that she is too "Westernized" to return to Sri Lanka, although she was delighted to get to know them and learn of their lives.

Manel can not determine which language is her mother tongue. Her parents and her relatives in Sri Lanka all speak English, but they are well aware that this is the colonizer's language. Manel's ambivalence about her language identification is due to speaking Swahili growing up with her African friends in Kenya and learning English and Singhalese (the language of Sri Lanka) from her parents, who spoke these at home. In Kenya, another language was added to her repertoire; since first grade her parents sent her to a French school. Manel feels she can talk about sex in any language. She discusses it frequently with many different people.

Manel, who dated African boys in Kenya, now dates a "White Southern boy." Previously, she dated an East Indian immigrant. However, she believes that

> South Asian men are too conservative and I am a feisty woman who needs a lot of space and respect. . . . My parents gave up the idea of arranging a marriage for me very early in my life. They knew I would not go for it.

Her father's racism became evident when she dated African men. In fact, her parents sent her to the United States to prevent her from doing so.

Manel's mother talked to her about sex "in a very scientific fashion"; she conversed mostly about menstruation, not sex.

> So I explored sex by myself, went out with a lot of guys [including an African teacher and a British student]. . . . My first sexual experience was with a teacher who was then about 23 and I was 16. I figured he could teach me something but it was a great disappointment. I have grown sexually since then and am very outgoing.

Manel feels that "it is as if I am three sexual people: one South Asian, the other African, and now also American."

Her aunts caution her that she would overwhelm a potential husband in Sri Lanka with her short hair, tattoo, and aggressive sexuality. She enjoys shattering the stereotype of the passive Asian woman. Yet she is flattered by the "exoticism" attributed to her by her White boyfriend. However, she granted that

> going out with a White man is stressful sometimes. I need to find a place for me in these interracial relationships. In a way the parts of me he does not understand are sources of power to me . . . [But] there are lots of things White men don't need to consider because of their privilege . . .

Because Manel and her family have migrated so many times and to so many disparate places, she feels the loneliness of never fully belonging and the angst of not knowing where to go back to feel at home.

> There is always a part of you that is not seen, recognized, or acknowledged. And of course, there are things about the lives of people here that I do not fully understand.

Despite her vibrant personality and positive outlook, Manel's statement illustrates the pain and loss associated with migration.

AYLA

I interviewed Ayla in her office. We spoke of many different things and shared tea before beginning the interview. Like some of the other women interviewed, Ayla came to the United States from Turkey to study for a graduate degree. After several years in the United States and a return trip to Turkey to gather data for her doctoral dissertation, "a job that provided a work permit fell on my lap." She decided to stay in the United States indefinitely. This was difficult to justify to her family. One relative asked her, "What are you doing there all alone? It is against nature for a woman to do that."

Although Ayla misses her family a great deal, she knows what life in Turkey as a married woman would entail; she has observed her sisters' and female cousins' lives. Since coming to the United States Ayla believes she has "come to [her] own authority." She fears that if she returned she would not be able to be her "own person" and would "[feel] cramped there."

The wave of Islamic religious fundamentalism sweeping Moslem countries worries her a great deal. She believes it has disastrous effects on women's lives, which she wants to avoid. Despite restrictions, a strong feminist contingent exists in Turkey. These women march against domestic violence and are very sophisticated about sexuality. There is even a contingent of out lesbians, yet they are not taken very seriously. Ayla developed a strong feminist consciousness since coming to the United States. In Turkey she had more of a Marxist perspective. Now she sees strong parallels between critiques of culture and gender. The two perspectives inform how she views the world. She learned the gender critique from her doctoral mentor. Because of these insights, she now respects her Turkish women role models more than before.

When Ayla grew up in Turkey, mothers did not speak about menstruation. She learned of this and other sexual topics from her peers, not her mother. She had sex once or twice during adolescence but never spoke to anyone about this. In fact, no one spoke about their sexual behavior.

> There were some "characters" that everybody knew were
> sleeping around and getting pregnant. One thing was to have
> a relationship and another to make yourself available to

everyone. In general, parents acted as if they were half blind and half deaf as long as you were discreet.

Ayla found that in the United States,

> it is imperative to talk about sex and sexuality if you want to make friends. I talk about these issues, but I am never comfortable or at ease with these topics.

Although Ayla matured sexually in Turkey and could speak in Turkish about sex, she prefers to talk about it in English. Even with her Turkish women friends, it is easier to speak in English about sexuality. Perhaps this is because "one has more practice and less prohibition talking about this in English." Yet she finds that in the United States there is not enough differentiation between what is sexual and what is sensual.

Although Ayla still defines herself as heterosexual, she is "toying with the idea" of falling in love with a woman. She has had "crushes" on women but never acted on them. It actually feels "like a gift" to know she can have "this fluidity." However, it also feels "gutsy and difficult to jump into lesbian relationships." Because she is not part of a tight Turkish community in the United States she does not worry about their (imagined) opinions or about gossip reaching her family in Turkey.

DENISE

Denise, an energetic 61-year-old French Canadian, was delighted to be interviewed. She actively pursued me to interview her after she had heard about my study and suggested the names of a few eager friends of hers. She came to the United States from Quebec City in the 1960s motivated by several factors: the weather, a good job, and a love affair. She comes from a large strict Catholic family in rural Quebec. Her mother valued education and ensured all her children spoke French correctly. Even though her family was poor while Denise matured, all the children finished school. This was atypical for families of her class and cultural background. Denise became a teacher because it was the cheapest way to get an education and a job.

She went through menarche when she was 10 years old and had

no idea what was happening to her. She got her sexual education from an older cousin "who knew everything." This cousin suggested she use tampons rather than napkins but her mother would not hear of it. Her mother thought that to have an object in the vagina was "perverted" and would make her daughter a "slut." This same cousin encouraged Denise to go out with boys when she was 14 or 15. But Denise was reserved. She wanted to be praised by the adults and saw that this cousin was always in trouble. Instead of going out with boys, Denise studied, first in French and later in English.

Denise finds that speaking about sex is easier to do in English than in French, probably because she has been in an English-speaking environment for many years. But her choice of language depends on who she is speaking to. Even though she prefers to use English to talk about sex, she prefers to use French during sexual intercourse because "French is more descriptive and has a better vocabulary for sex." She does not "experience the same depth of feeling when speaking in English."

Although I asked Denise several questions in French during the interview, she always responded in English with just a smattering of French. I found this all the more interesting because our conversations outside the interview have always been in both languages and frequently just in French.

All her life, Denise was interested in "foreigners." Her fascination was particularly intense with Jewish immigrants to Canada from European countries. She found Canadian Anglophones and French men too arrogant and French Canadian men very boring. In her 20s she had relationships with men from Europe and the Middle East. Her first relationship was with a Jewish man from Turkey. Finally, she fell in love with a Hungarian man who had immigrated to Canada shortly after the war. When he moved to the United States, she also moved. Their relationship has lasted more than 30 years, but they have not chosen to marry. Denise learned at an early age "to be an independent working woman" and was never "willing to sacrifice her independence for the love of any man." Denise observed her mother's, aunts', and later sisters' and cousins' lives. Because of what she saw, she has always had "a negative image of marriage."

Going through menopause was difficult for Denise because this lover of many years, who was less knowledgeable than she about sex when they first began their relationship, made insensitive comments. He told her "Your vagina is too dry." This was painful and irritating to hear. Nevertheless she continues to love him dearly even though they are not having sex now. Lately, Denise is aware of feeling less desire. She is aware she is aging, but she rejects a matronly self-image.

In the course of the interview, Denise volunteered that although she has good women friends, she has never wanted to be sexually involved with women.

In Northern California, I interviewed several women who had migrated to the United States from Latin American countries. Although they did not know each other, there are similarities in their stories. While there also are differences, their stories are grouped together because of their cultural and age similarities and because of the proximity in the timing and location of these interviews.

SOLEDAD

Soledad, born in Brazil, has lived in many different countries. Her father, a European Jew, migrated to Brazil as a young boy after World War II. Her Brazilian-born mother was also the daughter of European Jews. Her mother's family arrived in Brazil shortly before the War. They "Latinized" their surname; Soledad's father did not. In the 1980s, when Soledad was 13 years old, her family migrated to the United States for her father's job. Her parents have since returned to Latin America.

She identifies as

> a Latina lesbian who is also Jewish, but being Jewish is a very small part of my identity. That is why I use my mother's maiden name as part of my name, so people recognize I am Latina.

She describes her family as "a Jewish family with Catholic morals" because of the influence of Latin American culture on their lives.

Soledad's mother spoke to her occasionally about sex. Her comments amounted to "sex is dirty, sex is gross, sex is something you just do for a man." Soledad came out as a lesbian six years before the interview took place. She was very surprised to find herself in love with a woman because although I always felt kind of strange and weird and confused, I never had that sense others have that they knew they were lesbians since they were 5 years old. Part of it is because I am very "femmie"—or whatever you want to call it. The women I knew who identified as lesbians didn't look like me.

Soledad was in a relationship with a man she intended to marry when she fell in love with a woman. With this woman "everything felt right." She did not feel "strange and weird and confused" anymore. Soledad believes very strongly that the separation from her parents made it possible for her to come out.

None of Soledad's partners has ever spoken Portuguese or Spanish, which are the languages she spoke as a child. She loves to use endearments and nicknames in those two languages both when speaking to her partners and during sex.

They are made-up words that sound like Spanish or Portuguese but are not; you know, like "mimita" or "chucritita" or something like that. Even if they spoke the language they would have to get the meaning of my invented words from my nonverbal expressions, not from the actual words that don't really mean anything. Using these invented words makes me feel tender, though. Words in English, no matter how sweet, don't have the same effect.

For several years, Soledad offered training workshops on safe sex for lesbians. She had always presented these workshops in English. Once, she was asked to present in Spanish and as she was explaining in Spanish, the same things she had explained in English many times, she felt a sense of intense embarrassment "creeping up. It was like to say these things in Spanish was 'too public' and 'too cold.'"

The conversation with Soledad was held completely in Spanish, except when the topic was sexuality or lesbianism—then she preferred English. She was very articulate about the importance of her language choices and the impact of different languages in her life.

ROSA

Rosa comes from "a family of matriarchs (my mother, grandmother, aunts; we had no fathers or grandfathers)" in rural Nicaragua. Several relatives had immigrated to the United States and other parts of Latin America. This helped her mother's prompt decision to migrate with Rosa's oldest sister. Rosa, still a small child, was left with—and raised by—her grandmother for a few years. Political disturbances in Nicaragua under the Somoza dictatorship, not economic reasons, motivated the migration of her family members. After the 1972 earthquake in Nicaragua, her mother decided that political and natural disasters were overwhelming her family. Slowly, she managed to bring everyone to the United States despite the fact that her job was as a hotel maid, which left little money for necessities.

Rosa was delighted to come to the United States. Yet she was disappointed to find her mother had changed dramatically from "the sweet Latin mother I remembered." Her disappointment stemmed from the discovery that her mother had a boyfriend, which would have been unthinkable in Nicaragua.

> It was a shock to know she had a boyfriend; I guess she started thinking about herself and what she needed, not just about being a mother. I was a child, I could not understand my mother's new life.

Rosa, very sad, cried frequently but said nothing to anyone. A distinct disruption occurred when her mother invited her boyfriend to move into the apartment with them. Rosa had never lived with a man. It was extremely difficult for her to tolerate his presence and her mother's attention to him. When Rosa's mother died several years ago, "it felt like a tremendous loss. Like losing her for a second or third time, this time forever."

Initially, Rosa spoke no English and had trouble in school. Studying became her escape; it helped her forget her disappointment in her mother. Eventually, she graduated from high school and went on to college. Her quest for having boyfriends helped her forget the realities at home and her mother's emotional unavailability. But she did not have sex; she just "kissed and touched." When she was 18 she had intercourse for the first time with a White man 10 years her senior. She found the experience rather "difficult" because

> the whole thing was a let down. I had heard so much about it in the movies and on television that I hoped it was more than

it really was. Also, I was shocked to see that the man had so much control in the sexual act. I thought both the man and the woman had control. I also saw that the whole thing was very simple, not something great as I had previously thought.

Rosa became intimate with a college classmate after this man moved to another city. This second lover had never had sex before, so it was "strange to be with a man who knew so little." Adding to her disillusionment, this guy accused her of "giving him something in his private parts." Rosa became indignant and insisted he see a doctor at the hospital. The doctor said that she was perfectly healthy. The problem was "the guy had an allergic reaction to having sex with women." After the "diagnosis," he wanted to keep dating her. Rosa, however, had had enough of him.

After this misadventure, Rosa met the man she eventually married. "He is Jewish, a very gentle and spiritual man." They have two children and are very happy together. With her future husband, Rosa had sex for the first time with someone she truly loved. It made an enormous difference in the experience.

As a child in Nicaragua, Rosa learned about sex from her older sister's books. In the United States, she had sex education in the schools, but "all this was too scientific: anatomy, venereal diseases, how to get pregnant, but nothing about love." Her mother and her grandmother taught Rosa how to be a mother, not how to be a woman or a sexual person. In Nicaragua, the nuns at her school and the Catholic Church only spoke about procreation, never pleasure.

Rosa has only discussed sex in Spanish with her sister. She could not have spoken about this topic with a Latino man or with her mother. All her sexual partners have spoken only English, so all her conversations with them have been in English. She wonders what it would be like to make love with a Latino man, but assumes she will never have this experience as long as she is married. She intends to remain faithful to her husband.

LUCÍA

Lucía migrated twice to the United States from her native Perú. She first came at age 9 so her parents could attend a Midwestern graduate school. She spent 2 years in the United States, during which time she learned English and made friends. When her parents finished their education, the family returned to Perú. Several years later, amid a deep Peruvian economic crisis, her parents divorced. Her father returned permanently to the States with Lucía and her siblings. Her mother remained in Perú despite the country's financial problems. Before the move to the United States, Lucía attended a nun's school in Lima and hated the "rigidity" of that school; she longed for her American school and classmates. She gladly returned even though the migration meant separation from her mother. She has lived in the United States since then.

Lucía's repeated migrations left her with a sense of loss of which she was unaware until she recently began therapy. This was the first time she framed her depression in terms of earlier life losses.

Before Lucía left Perú, her mother conversed with her about sex. But her stepmother gave her the most salient information on these issues. She is a White woman, who married her father 3 years after the family permanently settled in the United States. She is fluent in Spanish. Lucía believes that had she stayed in Latin America with her mother, her experience of sexuality would have been very different. Yet she was at a loss to explain what those differences may have been.

Lucía has never been married and feels "in no rush" to do so, which was an interesting statement considering she was already 40 at the time of the interview. Her sexual experience is limited. She attributes this to her holding internally "all the Latin American ideals of getting married and having babies," but not having the external opportunity to live this. "I am morally a Latina. This is morally who I am, I have internalized that."

In college, Lucía had a best friend "who was also a very moral girl, and we supported each other in that." Lucía "lost [her] virginity at 20" to a Latino, but she was not in love with him. "It was more like just losing my virginity. I was 'in shock' for a long time after this happened." Several years after this incident, she met a man at work who was much older than she. Her parents knew about this and encouraged the relationship:

> They really were afraid I wasn't going to become sexually involved with any man. I don't know what was going through their heads. He asked me to spend the night in his apartment

and he was not divorced yet, so I called home to see what my parents thought and they said, "OK, take care of yourself, see you tomorrow." So I was in shock thinking, "My God, they are giving me away to this man!" I thought, of all the people in the world, why would they give me away to a married man? That was the weirdest message.... But it wasn't what I wanted because I could not really get married.

After that, Lucía had a significant relationship with an Irish man with whom she lived for 5 years. She believes that migration affected her sexuality because of the contradicting norms she experienced bridging the two cultures. She believes she "cannot be fully present" in a relationship with a man who is not Latino, which is why she experienced difficulties with her Irish boyfriend. It is hard for her to be in a relationship with someone who is monolingual. In addition,

> there are all these stereotypes about Latina women: You are a virgin, you are a good Catholic girl, you are so monogamous, but then when you get in bed you are sexually charged and go crazy on men. I cannot deal with that way of thinking. When I am having sex I am not going crazy, I am almost "directing the traffic" to make sure it is all fine and that makes it hard to relax.

Clearly, Lucía does not have an easy time with sexuality. Perhaps her cultural explanations for her difficulties are a screen to avoid dealing with more complex issues. Interestingly, she was eager to participate in the interview and spoke for more than 3 hours. She detailed her migration experience and sexual relationships. She seriously explored these issues during the interview and reflected carefully on her answers.

CORNELIA

Cornelia's interview, by contrast, was short and unembellished. She had also migrated with her family as a consequence of the financial crisis in Perú. Her father is Peruvian; her mother is French. Cornelia identifies deeply with her country of birth. She finds her mother's disparaging comments about Perú and Peruvians quite unnerving. She consented to emigrate from Perú because her father convinced her that her family needed her. Yet she feels her life has been interrupted by this unwanted migration. At interview time she was engaged to a Peruvian man who has lived in the United States for 15 years. She sees this relationship and future marriage as maintaining her connection to Perú and making her less afraid of American life.

Cornelia learned about sex in Perú "in the street, from strangers." Her knowledge did not come from sexual encounters but from conversations in Spanish with people she knew. Thus she feels at ease speaking about sex in Spanish, not English. She uses Spanish for important conversations and during sex with her fiancé. In fact, all of Cornelia's important relationships are with people who speak Spanish. I could not help but sense that Cornelia's strong attachment to Perú and to the Spanish language may have been influenced by her mother's rejection of Perú and her lack of interest in speaking Spanish—a second language for her mother, who now uses English in her daily life.

Even though Cornelia prefers everything Peruvian, her sexual life is better here because there are not so many restrictions:

> In Perú, you live at home with your parents until you get married. You do not live with your boyfriend. Here my mother and father have gotten used to it and accept that I am living with him. Also, after marriage women are supposed to stay at home and have sex only when their husbands want to. Here women have more of a say. The difference between men and women is not as marked here. In Perú a woman who steps out of her established role is criticized and rejected. The importance of virginity is changing there but it is all very clandestine and sex is accepted only if you marry the man you had sex with.

Had Cornelia remained in Perú, she wished she could have been a man to have more power and be able to do all the things that are "not appropriate for a young lady." But as she lives in the United States, she is adapting to life here. She expressed gratitude for the opportunity to try new things.

The three oldest interviewees, Judith, Rivka, and Liv, came to the United States in the 1930s, shortly before the beginning of World War II. The political events transpiring in Europe motivated their migrations. Both Judith and Rivka are of Jewish ancestry. Liv comes from an upper-class Scandinavian family.

JUDITH

Judith, the oldest of the three, came from Russia with her widowed mother and siblings after Russia was already a socialist country but still anti-Semitic despite revolutionary rhetoric. They obtained visas to Canada, and from Canada entered the United States. At the time of the interview she resided in the Midwest.

Upon arrival in the States, Judith started attending public school and learned English very quickly. She was "painfully shy" and did not speak at all in class. This led her teachers to think that perhaps she was unintelligent. Judith believed this about herself for many years, until after years of marriage and raising four children, she went back to college and received a bachelor's degree, summa cum laude.

Since childhood, Judith avoided speaking Russian. Her memories of her birth country were mostly painful and unpleasant. Her impoverished family suffered under the Soviet government's anti-Semitic policies. After her mother's death in the 1950s, Judith and her siblings all ceased to speak in Russian at all.

Right before the war, Judith married her high school sweetheart. He was a good-looking Jewish American who left almost immediately for his European war duty. She feared for his safety but he returned from the war unharmed. He lived into his late 70s and died peacefully at home.

Judith never talked about sex, even with her husband. She "just did what she needed to do." And since raising children was "a lot of fun," sex was "worth the effort." Judith's pictures as a young bride and mother reveal an attractive smiling woman. Our conversation was short: Judith was not particularly interested in recalling her migration or giving voice to silenced sexual issues. After her husband's death, her financial situation "is not so good," her children all live very far away, and she feels the effects of aging.

RIVKA

Rivka, on the other hand, was delighted to talk about her experiences. Her husband's recent death prompted memories of their relationship. She also willingly shared thoughts about her parents, leaving Europe, and many events surrounding the war.

Rivka is fluent in at least five languages. She acquired them as her family moved from country to country in Europe during her childhood, trying desperately to escape persecution. Finally, her father decided to migrate to America. They left Europe just in time, in early 1939.

In the United States, Rivka met and married a Jewish American man. Since she "knew nothing about sex before marriage," Rivka learned about sex in English from her husband. Still, "true emotions do not happen in English" for Rivka.

At the end of a long and lively conversation full of family stories and anecdotes about her childhood, marriage, and professional life, Rivka became silent. Then she said,

> You know, sometimes I wonder what I would have done with my life if I had been born in a different generation. The idea of lesbianism, for example, never crossed my mind when I was young. Considering my commitment to women's issues, I wonder what I would have done if I had known there were alternatives.

This comment caught me by surprise, because all along she had been speaking very positively about her married life and about how much she missed her husband. Apparently, for her, musings about "what could have been" include issues of sexual orientation.

LIV

From a very early age, Denmark-born Liv decided that she was not going to leave too many "what could have been" questions unanswered. Her life is a saga of changes. She tested all sorts of things, prime among them drug experimentation. This is surprising, considering that this was a time when drug use was not common, particularly among people of her generation.

Liv came to the United States at the beginning of her adolescence in the 1930s with her father, an American diplomat, and her aristocratic mother. Her father, aware of the dangerous events transpiring in Europe, requested a transfer to the United States to avoid dangers and protect his wife and children.

Her first years in the States were very difficult for Liv because she "could not understand American children's behavior: They were rude to their teachers and rough with each other, even the girls." She had difficulty getting along with peers, who made fun of her for her "quaint European ways." Language, however, was not a problem. She had grown up speaking both Danish and English at home; she had also learned French and German in school.

While she was still an adolescent, Liv's parents died in rapid succession, shortly after the war's end. She thought briefly of returning to Europe but decided that it would be foolish to reenter a continent ravaged by war. At this time, wealthy, young, orphaned, alone, and confused, she started using drugs.

Eventually, Liv married. She stopped using drugs when she became pregnant because she was aware of fetal health dangers, yet she resorted to alcohol. Several decades, marriages, and children later, a middle-aged Liv became "clean and sober." She has remained so for more than 20 years. Liv became involved with a woman after committing to sobriety, raising her children to adulthood, and divorcing for the third time. Since then she has lived a lesbian life and considers herself "happy and adjusted."

She said little about language or her sexual life. Her conversation was focused upon her successful life transformations. She identified these as overcoming addiction, alcoholism, and the lack of family support and cultural identity she experienced in her youth.

The stories of Roya, Mina, Colleen, Violeta, Nora, and Annette emerged from a study that explored the experiences of women who were separated from their mothers between the ages of 12 and 22. Their separations were due to international migration. The reasons for the migration and separation from their mothers include economic hardship, political upheaval, and marriage and job opportunities. Their ages ranged from 23 to 60 at the time of the interviews.

These narratives evolved through an in-depth interview format that explored the psychological impact of premature separation on mother-daughter relationships and on the daughter's psychological development. Interview questions tapped participants' experiences with the migratory process, its impact on their relationship with their mothers, and their development as women. As in the other two studies, the interviews were taped and transcribed. The transcribed interviews were subsequently analyzed thematically. All interviewees in this study expressed satisfaction with the opportunity to discuss major life events that they had seldom talked about.

ROYA

Roya was 23 years old at the time of the interview. She came to the United States from Iran at 16 to live with her husband, whom she met upon arrival. She had not been back to Iran during the intervening years. Roya felt emotionally supported by her husband and his family in her transition, but it was not the same as her own parents' support. Many times she silenced herself with them because she felt alienated from her new surroundings but did not want to upset them. Despite their kindnesses, Roya felt compelled to become self-reliant emotionally.

The hardest adjustment for Roya was "the difficulty that people in this country seem to have about getting closer to each other. People here are more emotionally distant and friendships don't come so easily." Because of the difficulty she experienced making friends, Roya felt closer to her husband and her in-laws. This caused, in turn, greater distance from her own mother.

> I grew differently than I would have had I stayed in my country. I became a different person. . . . Now I am very different from my mom. . . . I think I also may have felt some resentment because I felt like blaming her for allowing me to leave the country when I did. . . . Although she actually did something that was good for me. She was thinking about the best thing for my life. So I couldn't really blame her and yet I couldn't help myself.

Roya adamantly stated that her arranged marriage was not forced upon her. She did not understand why in the United States the two were seen as synonymous. Indeed, her husband was young, handsome, kind, and loving toward her. Had she been afforded the opportunity to freely choose the man she would marry, it is likely she would have chosen her husband or someone very much like him. Far from being problematic, her husband and her marriage were her sources of support in the United States. The sources of her distress emanated from her mother's absence and the loss of all other familiar relationships, customs, and places.

When she first arrived in the United States she attended a community college to learn English and further her education. At this time, her clothing reflected her religious and cultural background and, as a married woman, she covered her hair. After a few months, she grew tired of the teasing her head scarf provoked and, after a conversation with her husband, they agreed she would dress "American." Once again, support came from her husband—the hurt and difficulties came from the reactions of people in the host society.

Roya, informed by her own adjustment difficulties, believes she would not let a daughter of hers "go away because it would be too hard for her to move at a young age with new people around and not having her own family around."

This is a consistent response from these women. They tended to see positive consequences to their migration. Most framed the pain of separation as a positive force that fostered their independence and autonomy. However, when asked if they would let their daughters migrate under similar circumstances, those who had the hardest time adjusting were more protective and less willing. All agreed they would prefer their daughters undergo this experience at a later age than they had.

MINA

Like Roya, Mina is Iranian. She was 28 years old at the time of the interview and was expecting her first child. She had come to the United States several years before to study; her family sought to protect her from the Iranian Revolution's upheaval by sending her to study abroad. She met her husband, who is also Iranian, in the United States.

Mina, who is not very talkative, spoke reluctantly about her experiences. However, she described herself as lucky in her marriage and very happy anticipating her upcoming motherhood. She expressed strong dislike for the possibility that her child would have to experience migration at an early age. She dreaded the prospect of ever being apart from her child. Another hesitation was her desire for her child to be knowledgeable about cultural customs and values before being separated from parents by migration.

COLLEEN

Colleen, initially separated from her mother in rural Ireland when barely 12 years old, was sent to Dublin to work as a domestic to help support her family. At 14, she was sent alone, again, to the United States to work as live-in domestic help. Her family's poverty meant she sent her wages home. She felt very sad and lonely forced to live away from her mother. One of her life regrets is never having enough time with her now deceased mother. Colleen married an Irish American man, bore several children, and continued to work to help support her family both in Ireland and the United States.

The hardest part of Colleen's migration experience was the loneliness: "No emotional support existed. If and when you cried, you cried alone." During the hardest years of her adolescence, Colleen found refuge in being "very devoted to church." Until she got married she "lived a very quiet single life, always knowing right from wrong, even though I was alone and on my own." In other words, she did not live a sexually active life before marriage even though there was no one to prevent her from doing so. She also says that she "could have gotten into alcohol, but did not." Her faith seems to have operated as a moral code and a protection from possible "lax" behavior.

Despite the pain and loneliness she endured, the distance afforded by the migration allowed her "to speak my mind and be outspoken. If I had never left Ireland, I would never have been able to do that."

Colleen's mother expressed regret to her adult daughter and said repeatedly that she wished she had not let her "go off to work at 12." Colleen philosophically mused, "But I realize work was part of life and there were really few choices."

VIOLETA

Violeta, 51 at the time of the interview, left Cuba in 1961. Her separation from her mother occurred first upon leaving Cuba and again a year later when she left her parents in the United States and went to Canada to work and study. Upon returning to the United States to stay permanently, Violeta fell in love with a woman and started living as a lesbian. Years later, she came out to her mother, who responded to her in an unexpectedly warm and supportive way. Before migration her relationship with her mother had been very strained and continued to be so for many years. After her coming out, however, their relationship became progressively warmer. Violeta attributes the improvement to changes within her mother and to her mother's affection for Violeta's partner. As Violeta has aged, she has learned to see her mother as a woman whose life was limited by being a woman of her generation and culture; this made Violeta more understanding. Her mother, in turn, has learned to express more love and caring as she ages.

In the first few years after migration Violeta felt "a tremendous sense of loneliness." It was made tolerable because she "prayed a lot and made some good friends." That is why—though Violeta does not have any children—she could not imagine letting her own child go alone to another country. "It would be too hard to do," she says, speaking from the memories of her own experience.

NORA

At the age of 17—43 years before the interview—Nora came to the United States from Cuba to live with her aunt and uncle for a year while she attended high school. During her intended short stay she learned English, met an American, married him, and never returned to Cuba. Her mother eventually joined her in the United States 30 years later; she had died a few months prior to the interview. The recent death of her mother made it very difficult for Nora to speak about her; she could not do so without tears.

When she arrived in the United States Nora found it hard to adjust to the new customs, particularly the food. While she had learned English in Cuba, she found everyday American pronunciation was very different from what she had been taught in Cuban schools. Now, after having lived most of her life in the United States, Nora cannot imagine what her life in Cuba would have been like. Her extended family now lives in the United States, which makes her feel that she has the best of both worlds.

ANNETTE

Annette heard me talk informally about the mother-daughter study. She clamored to tell me her story. Although not included in the original group of interviews, her story is relevant nonetheless. It provides yet another cultural context that created early geographical separation between a mother and daughter.

Annette left East Germany secretively in the 1950s. She went to West Berlin to study what she wanted to rather than have her choices determined by official policies. She left without telling her parents. Her sense of guilt for abandoning them was excruciating for her. She did not tell them anything in an attempt to protect them; she did not want to burden them with a secret that could create political difficulties.

After her secret departure she contacted her mother to let her know her whereabouts. Her mother, initially upset, eventually forgave Annette for leaving without notice. They initiated a very active correspondence that continued uninterrupted for 30 years until her mother's death.

The initial adjustment was hard because Annette had no money, but it was empowering because she was able to do what she wanted: study. Her mother had taught her to love books and ideas, and one of Annette's sorrows was that she could not talk to her mother about all she learned. She finally saw her mother again (for 2 weeks) after 15 years of separation. But, obviously, that visit was inadequate to exchange all the feelings, ideas, and knowledge Annette had accumulated. The letters they exchanged were also inadequate for all she wished to discuss with her mother. Government policies in East Germany impaired their communication as well:

> My mother knew English and I would have loved to send her journals and books but that was prohibited by the East German government. The irony is that now that the borders are open, she is dead.

Beyond the intellectual interests, Annette yearned to talk with her mother about her American husband, her new country, and things of importance to her. The brief visits she was allowed to make to East Germany while her mother was alive were always "intense and beautiful." They helped her "preserve some of the illusions and memories of childhood." But she could not visit often, because of the many limitations the East German government placed on travel. She lovingly and nostalgically recounted minute details of those visits, down to the kind of wine they drank, what food her mother cooked, and the color of the tablecloth.

Even though we had a lengthy conversation, it was clear that she had much more to say about the regrets she felt for the opportunities she and her mother had missed. At the same time, she was also clear that she did not regret leaving East Germany and she "would do it all over again." She found the interview "upsetting, because it brought so much back . . . the pain and the price to be paid." And yet, she was glad I gave her "the opportunity to do this."

The next two narratives were part of a preliminary study on the impact of immigration on adolescent development. For this project, several immigrant adolescents were interviewed. An open-ended, relatively unstructured interview format was used in these interviews. Study participants were asked to talk generally about their migration experiences and their aftermath. Additional questions clarified how immigration had affected their personal identity, cultural identification, peer relations, and other important problems and issues. The participants were all high school seniors. All had migrated during adolescence rather than during childhood. All were fluent in English while still knowledgeable of their first language.

Novena's and Iris's stories provide poignant insights into the experience of young women's migration in the midst of adolescence. Both narratives are articulate and sophisticated. Clearly both Novena and Iris had reflected upon their experiences and tried to make sense of them, which is why these two narratives were chosen to be included here. Their two stories are rich in unique characteristics of how they interpret their experiences. The dissimilarities between Novena's and Iris's coping styles add to our understanding of women immigrants in general and adolescent immigrants in particular.

NOVENA

Novena, a Jewish Russian immigrant, was 17 at the time of the interview. She presented herself as a subdued, mature young woman. She was preoccupied applying to various universities, which meant spending little time socializing with her peers. She preferred to spend time conversing with adult friends. She spoke slowly, carefully, and "correctly." Novena found the immigration 4 years previous both "hard and exciting." She characterized her subsequent adaptation as smooth.

She also described a sense of loss in leaving behind Russian friends and relatives. She was particularly pained to leave her grandparents, who had raised her since she was little. She came to live with her parents and siblings, and she experienced difficulty adjusting to the new family constellation.

At the same time there was the excitement of a new world and travel. She felt that coping with the changes brought on by immigration made her more mature than her peers because she was forced into an "analysis of life around me." She also was confronted with massive difference—"the language, sights, sounds." As a consequence, she "grew a lot at that time."

When Novena arrived in the United States, she entered into an already established Russian immigrant community. It provided a transition group that eased the adjustment process. Although the first year was made easier by this group, the second year she was forced to confront the dominant culture more directly, which caused difficulties. She felt conflicted about her identity as a Russian and the need to adjust to life in her new country. She decided to "Americanize" after a difficult year because she had been "very depressed with her differences from others." This was compounded by her increasing difficulty in relating to Russians.

Novena's parents, like many other immigrant parents, became dependent on their children to negotiate the new language and social norms. They leaned on her to function in American society. They could not understand her desire to leave home. Her relationship with her boyfriend also caused friction between them. They worried about her being "too close" to her boyfriend because she saw him almost every day. Her boyfriend, although also Russian, had been in the United States since an early age and did not behave "Russian enough" for her parents' taste. In her words:

it is hard because I live in one dimension and my parents live
in another. Our goals are different. I could never live the life
my mother has lived, nor could I do it in this country even if
I tried to.

When Novena expresses these feelings to her parents, her mother
cries and "feels devalued" by her daughter. Novena tried to convince
her mother of her love for her. She emphasized how she valued her
mother's support and caring. But "it is hard to convince my parents
that I love them when they think they are being rejected." She found
it difficult to convey to her parents her desire to "take advantage of
new life in the U.S., even if it means engaging in behavior they disap-
prove of."

Novena's parents seem to be having a hard time while her adjustment seems fairly smooth. Were it not for their difficulties, Novena's
immigration appears to be mostly a positive experience.

IRIS

Iris, also 17, migrated to the United States from Israel 3 years prior to
the interview. Her family migrated for her father's job as a physics
professor at a prestigious university. She dressed casually in jeans,
sneakers, and a sports jacket. She was quite shy initially but spoke
adamantly when presenting her own opinions. Iris missed Israel a
great deal and found adjustment to the United States very difficult.
She looked forward to returning home. After 3 years in the same
school she spoke to none of her classmates. This was due, in part, to
initial language difficulties and to her dislike of the other students.
When she socialized, she did so only among a small group of Israeli
students.

Her tone of voice became quite angry when she talked about how
much better Israelis receive immigrants than do Americans. She said
those who want to talk to her only want to argue about Palestinian
politics. She clearly rejected the host culture, despite speaking near
perfect English. She did not date Americans, Jewish or not. This
limited her choices since there were few Israelis available. She
rejected girlfriends because "American girls are superficial and too
much into boys and clothes and makeup. " When she first arrived in
the United States she had an Israeli friend but this girl

"Americanized" quickly. She started making American friends and wearing makeup and high heels. This did not pull me. I go where and how I want and I don't care what other people think. American girls throw themselves on the boys. I am Israeli, that's why I liked this Israeli girl because we could talk about everything. But when she changed I did not want to be friends anymore with any other girl.

Iris described feeling completely isolated and lonely. She attributed these feelings to her "refusal to become Americanized." Contrary to most children of immigrants, her refusal to "Americanize" caused conflicts with her mother. Her mother felt Iris's stance prevented her from taking advantage of her new life in this country.

Iris was eagerly awaiting the opportunity to join the Israeli army. She looked forward to her family's scheduled return home in 2 years. She hoped this would be the time when she would find a boyfriend. However, in her visits to Israel, Iris had been disappointed, particularly by some of her former girlfriends. She found them too preoccupied with their boyfriends and not attentive enough to their obligatory military service.

Although I would not presume to put words in her mouth or to define her identity for her, it seems possible that Iris was confused about her sexual orientation. Some of what she left unsaid points in that direction. She presented her refusal to date men, Jewish or not, in cultural terms. But she never had a boyfriend in Israel before coming to the United States. Thoughts of her future military service are more attractive to her than the thought of "datable" Israeli men. Her claim that she would only date Israelis seems to provide a safety mechanism to avoid heterosexual dating altogether. Although she idealized her life in Israel, she never spoke of truly liked friends of either sex left behind. Perhaps when she returned to Israel, as she hoped to do in the next few years, she confronted some issues that she was not ready to tackle at this point in her life.

These narratives illustrate the commonalities and differences women experience during and following immigration. As the women told their stories, the importance of patterns of language usage, the mother-daughter relationship, and issues of sexuality emerged as powerful themes. Even when they were not the central topic of an interview, these three themes were present in one form or another for all of the narratives. The significance of these three major themes to women's experience of immigration will be the subject of following chapters.

Migration, Sexuality, and the Preservation of Culture and Tradition

4

> S exuality seems to have a revolutionary
> potential so strong that many political
> women and men are afraid of it. They
> prefer, therefore, to dismiss its importance
> by arguing that it is not as central as other
> factors, such as economic and political
> determination. . . . [However,] sexuality is
> much more central to social and political
> problems . . . than previously thought, and
> . . . unless a sexual revolution is incorpo-
> rated into political revolution, there will be
> no real transformation of social relations.
> (Accad, 1991, p. 237)

In most societies in the world, sexuality and sexual behavior are considered private matters and thus not central to political and social transformations. But, as we know, sexuality is not private (e.g., Brettell & Sargent, 1993; Caplan, 1987; Foucault, 1981; Laqueur, 1990; Parker et al., 1992; Valverde, 1985), which explains why so many cultures and countries try to control and legislate it. Indeed, as one historian observed, "sexual behavior (perhaps more than religion) is the most highly symbolic activity of any society. To penetrate [*sic!*] the symbolic system implicit in any society's sexual behavior is therefore to come closest to the heart of its uniqueness" (Trumbach, 1977, p. 24).

Sexuality is a universal component of human experience, yet how it is embodied and expressed is not. As anthropological, historical, and literary studies contend, "sexuality is culturally variable rather than a timeless, immutable essence" (Parker et al., 1992, p. 4). Even what is considered to be sexual or not in one cultural context is often strikingly different for people in another cultural environment.

The study of women's experiences reveals a variety of sexual and gender expectations across cultures. These cultural constructs inextricably inform the expression of female sexuality. Cultural traditions, colonial and other forms of social oppression, national identity, and the vicissitudes of the historical process inform the development and perception of female sexuality. These definitions carry a strong weight—if not altogether conscious—for both lesbians and heterosexual women. Definitions of what constitutes appropriate behavior for women are justified in the name of a society's prevalent values: nationalism, religion, morality, health, science, and so forth. Worldwide, women are enculturated and socialized to embody their sexual desire or lack thereof through their particular culture's ideals of virtue. The social group's expectations are inscribed in women's individual desire and expressed through their sexuality (Jaggar & Bordo, 1989). These definitions are strongly influenced by male sexual pleasure. Too often, women's expression of their own sexuality are silenced or condemned and its meaning interpreted by others, who deauthorize the woman's interpretation of her experience. The expectation of conformity to society's sexual norms exercise pressures on all women's sexuality—regardless of sexual orientation—in ways that do not burden most men.[1] Women's reproductive capacities are frequently appropriated by the state to establish its control over both citizens and territories. Historically, warriors have celebrated victories and consoled the frustrations of defeat through the forceful possession of women's bodies: War and rape are deeply connected.

Many immigrant communities carry concepts of familial or national honor and dignity that are strongly tied to women's sexual purity. Many of these communities instill a conservative and limited view of women's sexuality. These views also co-create and foster myths of male superiority.

This is why struggles surrounding acculturation in immigrant and refugee families center frequently on issues of daughters' sexual behaviors and women's sex roles in general. It is no secret that religious leaders are rather preoccupied with women's sexuality. All over the world, we are witnessing how "women, their role, and above all their control, have become central to the fundamentalist agenda" of Protestants, Catholics, Muslims, and others (Yuval-Davis, 1992, p. 278). Indeed, the great religions of the world uphold similar principles insofar as the submission of women to men is expected and decreed as "natural" or as divine law (Sahgal & Yuval-Davis, 1992).

As sociologist Nira Yuval-Davis (1992) argued

> The "proper" behaviour of women is used to signify the difference between those who belong to the collectivity and those who do not. Women are also seen as "cultural carriers" of the collectivity who transmit it to the future generation, and the "proper" control of women in terms of marriage and divorce ensures that children who are born to those women are not only biologically but also symbolically within the boundaries of the collectivity. (p. 285)

And "the proper behaviour of women" is usually equated with their fulfillment of traditional gender roles and their sexual behavior.

Immigration and the Body: Clothes and Sexuality

The psychological transformations demanded by the process of migration are inscribed in women's bodies through changes in hairstyles, clothes, and physical forms of behavior, including sexual behavior. The body-centeredness of sexuality gives rise to anxieties over the control of women's bodies and their sexuality in immigrant communities. A "freer" sexuality is commonly associated with modernity. The valorization of sexual pleasure in modern Western societies becomes both liberating and restrictive to women immigrants. It increases their options and opens new doors to self-fulfillment but it increases patriarchal concerns about and restrictions on women's sexual behavior in the new society. Many of these anxieties and concerns about women's bodies and their sexuality are expressed through concerns about women's clothes.

The significance of women's clothes is made evident by the primacy given to the issue of the veil by the ideologues of Islamic revolutions (Tohidi, 1991). Clothing restrictions imposed on women in the name of religion, tradition, or patriotism can be effective instruments of women's oppression. These types of clothing restrictions are usually not imposed on men. Paradoxically, they may be used by women themselves as an instrument of resistance (Fernea & Fernea, 1995; Odeh, 1993). "Behind the anonymity of the veil women can go about unrecognized and uncriticized" (Fernea & Fernea, 1995, p. 289). In other words, "clothing has special meaning for people who wear it that strangers may not understand" (Fernea & Fernea, 1995, p. 285).

In March 1994 a new exhibition, *Becoming American Women: Clothing and the Jewish Immigrant Experience, 1880–1920,* opened at the Chicago Historical Society. In the book that accompanies the exhibition, Barbara Schreier (1994), its conceptualizer and curator, recounted her early interest in this study of clothing and acculturation. When she interviewed first- and second-generation immigrants about the years of adjustment to U.S. society, "everyone had a clothing story" (p. 2). She concluded that clothing and acculturation mirror each other closely. "Clothing," she argued, is "an identifiable symbol of a changing consciousness" (p. 5):

> The decision to focus [the exhibition] on women was based on the long-standing relationship women have had with their appearance. Issues of dress unified women and framed their experience of life separate from men. . . . Even though men considered issues [of clothing], they did not record them with the same iconographic vocabulary as did women (p. 8).

Schreier noted further that "female immigrants discuss clothing in their memoirs, oral histories, and correspondence as pivotal markers of their journey and remembered objects of desire" (p. 9).

Historical circumstances a century later revealed similar parallels involving a vastly different culture. Anne Woollett and her collaborators (1994), in their research on Asian women's ethnic identity, noted "frequent associations of dress with ethnic identity" (p. 124) and observed that

> while dress is seen as an important aspect of ethnic identity by almost all the women interviewed . . . men's choice of clothing was rarely mentioned in the interviews. . . . Clothes would appear to have different significance for women as compared with men, and given that most studies have not focused upon women, may explain why dress is rarely used as a measure of ethnic identity in much of the literature. (Woollett et al., 1994, p. 125)

Woollett and her colleagues stated that because "the impact of gender on the representations of ethnic identity is not frequently or adequately considered" (p. 120), acculturation as expressed through women's clothing is usually ignored.

These authors astutely observed the importance women assign to their clothing and appearance as a statement of their relation to acculturation. Yet they did not question why it is so. We know that women—in Western culture as well as in other cultures—are coerced by patriarchal norms to define themselves through physical appearance. Women are equated with their bodies.

Connections and frictions between mothers and daughters, even without the tensions created by acculturation, are mediated by clothing, fashion, weight, and other appearance issues (Kaschak, 1992).

Women's preoccupation with clothing and appearance is closely associated with sexuality. Heterosexual standards of sexual attractiveness are not the only ones expressed through clothing; lesbian preoccupation with dress codes, whether the "politically correct" jeans and sneakers or "lipstick lesbians" fashion outfits, are an expression of concern with sexual attractiveness. Forms of expression may vary among different groups and generations of lesbians, but clothes and sexual attractiveness are pivotal for lesbians as well as heterosexual women.

Interestingly, the historical period on which the Chicago Historical Society exhibition focuses coincides with a period of intense public preoccupation with young women's sexuality. This was an era when large numbers of young, immigrant, unmarried women living in American cities were gainfully employed (Nathanson, 1991) and spent their time away from parental scrutiny. Schreier (1994) found lengthy editorials in the Jewish press admonishing these young working women not to use their savings to buy frivolous items of clothing. Similarly, many a family conflict stemmed from parental anger with daughters who bought coveted items of clothing with their meager wages rather than contributing further to the family's resources.

Schreier found in the case of Jewish immigrants to the United States at the beginning of the twentieth century that "contemporary observers did not pay as much attention to male plumage; even when they did, their words lack the moralistic, beseeching, and condemnatory tones with which they addressed women" (1994, p. 9).

Conversely, then as now, women resisted domination from both the larger society and their own communities through the use of clothing and other forms of resistance. The new freedom young, ethnically diverse, immigrant women acquired as wage earners expressed itself not only through the clothes they wore, but also in their refusal to accept chaperones and other forms of parental control over their sexuality (Ruiz, 1992). These young immigrant women clearly felt their lives were enhanced by their participation in the public sphere and by transcendence of the limitations they confronted within the private sphere of their homes and families.

These issues continue to be expressed in our time. Immigrant women's identity conflicts and identity transformations still are manifested through clothing and sexuality (Espín, 1984, 1987b, 1997). For parents, young women, husbands, and wives, dressing American or preserving traditional clothing styles can be grounds for intergenerational and marital conflict. But clothes can also become an expression of the whole family's transformation. Roya's husband's and in-laws' approving and encouraging her to abandon her head scarf is an illustration of this point.

The "Virtuous" Immigrant Woman: Women's Sexuality and Male Superiority

Some immigrants transplant the invented virtuous woman from their homeland and seek to control women's lives in the new country to preserve the ideal. The dichotomous construction of the "purity of our women" versus the notion of the "promiscuous White women" serves to maintain ethnic pride. Yet it also severely limits the personal expression of immigrant women.

Policing women's bodies and sexual behavior becomes for immigrant communities the main means of asserting moral superiority over the host culture. Women's choices are limited and curtailed to ensure women's virtue. By elevating immigrant women's chastity, masculinist and patriarchal power is reinforced in the name of the greater ideals of honor and national pride.

For many immigrant women, emphasis on self-renunciation and maintaining sexual purity is a primary determinant of their sexuality. Many of them still deem shunning sexual pleasure virtuous (e.g., Bonierbale et al., 1981; Espín, 1984). They regard sexual behavior exclusively as an unwelcome obligation toward their husbands and a necessary evil to create children. Some immigrant women express pride at their own lack of sexual pleasure or desire, and their negative attitudes toward sex are frequently reinforced by men's inconsiderate behavior and demands.

In these times of the global HIV epidemic, women's subordination of their sexual needs to those of men and lack of communication concerning women's sexual needs and desires can have disastrous results.

Other virtues like "dedication to family and husband" place a great burden on married women's shoulders by encouraging the expectation that they will be transmitters of culture at all costs. Family and cultural celebrations translate into long hours of cooking and house tending. Daughters are expected to help mothers in these tasks, further constraining their activities and free time. Sons are frequently free to go and enjoy celebrations without the expectation that they will help with the tasks at hand.

Another consequence of cultural support for beliefs in male superiority and women's and children's subordination, although not always specifically sexual, may also be disastrous. Women and children are seen as the suitable recipients for oppressed men's displaced anger, which can lead to abuse in the form of wife beating, incest, or rape. The situation is particularly tragic for women who may have limited linguistic abilities and may be totally dependent on their husbands for their livelihood and their legal status in the United

States.[2] "Immigrant community leaders, who are most often men, frequently deny the domestic abuse prevalent in their communities" (Narayan, 1995, p. 110). Even if this displacement of anger is understandable in the individual cases of immigrant men who may feel deeply frustrated in their new environment, it is unacceptable to justify it in the name of culture. Acceptance of violence against women as men's legitimate reaction to oppression is mysogynist and immoral.

Conversely, much is made about the incidence of male dominance in immigrant cultures by individuals in the host culture. However, it is important to remember that any expression of male dominance among immigrants is the specific culture's version of the myth of male superiority that exists in most cultures, including mainstream American culture.

Although many immigrants still subscribe to the traditional ideas of male superiority and its consequent forms of expression, many reject it outright. We must remember that there are many immigrant women who are actively involved in the feminist movement and who are unwilling to submit to the authority of male relatives. For example, the stories of Rivka, Mei, and Lin as well as the stories of the lesbian interviewees illustrate this point. Indeed, the existence and prevalence of lesbians and feminists among immigrants challenges the myth of the submissive immigrant woman that is prevalent in mainstream American culture.

Immigrant women's sexuality and behavior are not static. The established norms for women's appropriate sexual behavior undergo many transformations. For example, sociologist Yolanda Prieto (1992) found that immigrant Cubans' views of sexuality have changed drastically. The Cuban women and men she interviewed in New Jersey attributed these changes to cultural needs for women to work outside the home to contribute to the family income. The influence of the women's liberation movement in American society was a second strong influence. Virginity, which had been so central to the definition of a "good woman" in previous generations, is presently less important. Most of the mothers Prieto interviewed did not expect their daughters to be virgins until marriage. The mothers may have been truly accepting, resigned to the situation, or convinced that these are new times. Most of them perceived that the sexual revolution was here to stay; it was not just an anomaly of American society but rather "a state of the world." Still, despite these shifts in attitude, the area of female sexuality continues to be the most conflictual for these immigrant families.

Almost all of the interviewees in my studies actively attributed the transformations in their sexuality to their migration. These transformations included behaviors as diverse as coming out as lesbians, decisions concerning marriage and heterosexual relationships, and choices of clothing styles. Not all of these women were fully comfortable with their sexuality—but then, sex is not unproblematic for most women. Sex and sexuality can be a source of fear, pain, and embarrassment, and they can also be a source of happiness, pleasure, and fulfillment. In this, the interviewees are no exception.

The late poet Audre Lorde spoke of the power of the erotic in women's lives. Lorde, a Black, lesbian feminist immigrant from the Caribbean, wrote:

> Our erotic knowledge empowers us, becomes a lens through which we scrutinize all aspects of our existence, forcing us to evaluate those aspects honestly in terms of their relative meaning within our lives. And this is grave responsibility, projected from within each of us, not to settle for the convenient, the shoddy, the conventionally expected, nor the merely safe. (1984, p. 57)

According to Lorde, "In order to perpetuate itself, every oppression must corrupt or distort those various sources within the culture of the oppressed that can provide energy for change" (p. 53). One such source is women's erotic energy. She encourages all "women . . . to examine the ways in which our world can be truly different" (p. 55). This necessitates, for women, not being afraid of "the power of the erotic." "Once we know the extent to which we are capable of feeling that sense of satisfaction and completion, we can then observe which of our various life endeavors bring us closest to that fullest" (p. 54). Lorde sees the reclaiming of the erotic as an essential step in the process of developing healthy identities and struggling against racism.

For immigrant women, claiming their own sexuality becomes a necessary endeavor; it is a statement of their personhood, independent from the expectations of both their communities and American society. It would be naive, however, to ignore the fact that greater freedom may bring greater danger. "Sexuality in a male dominated society inevitably involves danger for women" (Caplan, 1987, p. 9). Rape and other forms of violence may become favored strategies to enforce submission at times of transition.

Like gender, sexual relations are political and socially constructed. The transformations of immigrant women's sexuality and gender roles imply political transformations and the construction of new gender norms for their communities. They also imply transformations for the host culture when it is confronted with new possibilities for female sexual expression.

The narratives reported in Chapter 3 show us how each of these women engaged in this transformative project. In some cases they were not fully aware of the process; it happened almost in spite of them. In others, they were consciously and purposefully involved in their own transformation. Indeed, it is almost as if these women felt compelled to transform themselves in their most private and intimate layers.

The transformations in their sexuality did not occur independently from other identity transformations, but rather were part of a process characterized by a move toward greater autonomy in all areas of their lives. Language changes became central to the transformation of identity as we will discuss in the next chapter.

Notes

1. This is not to say that gay men's sexuality is not subjected to conscious and unconscious controls by society.
2. Ironically, many of these husbands are not immigrants but U.S.-born citizens, and many are White.

5 | Language: Identity, Silence, and Sexuality

Language loss and its concomitant sense of identity loss and transformation are perhaps the
most powerful components of the immigrant experience. In her autobiographical account of migration, *Lost in Translation*, writer Eva Hoffman (1989)
vividly describes the intensity of this experience for
immigrants:

> Linguistic dispossession is. . . close to the
> dispossession of one's self . . . [There is a
> feeling that] this language is beginning to
> invent another me . . . [And] there is, of
> course, the constraint and the self-
> consciousness of an accent that I hear but
> cannot control. (p. 121)

Extensive discussion of the affective and cognitive implications of bilingualism and language
change is beyond the scope of this book. However,
these issues were central to my research questions
because they are extremely important for immigrants. Language—the forced learning of the new
and the loss of the old linguistic community—is
central to the migration experience as the responses

given by the interviewees in my study demonstrate. Language change is one of the most difficult problems the immigrant faces.

Beyond allowing the immigrant to function in the new context, a new language has profound impact on the immigrant's sense of self and identity, as Hoffman's statements illustrate. The immigrant learns "to live in two languages"; at the same time, she learns to live in two social worlds. Learning to "live" in a new language is not merely an instrumental process; it is not a neutral act. It implies becoming immersed in the power relations of the specific culture that speaks the specific language. Speaking with a foreign accent places one in a less privileged position within those power relations.

> Even supposing that the immigrant is in a country where his [/her] own language is spoken (although it can never be the exact same language), his [/her] speech act will take place at a particular moment of time and in a distinctive set of circumstances different from those he [/she] has known. (Grinberg & Grinberg, 1984, p. 100)

"One of the primary places where issues of national culture and family coherence come together is the question of language" (Bammer, 1994, p. 96). This issue becomes further complicated when different generations within a family have different levels of proficiency in the different languages spoken. While the first language or mother tongue may be taken to mean the native language of the mother, in the case of immigrants and refugees, children may be more fluent in the language of the host culture—which is really their first language rather than the language their mothers speak best (Bammer, 1994). In other words,

> language can play a complex role, both binding and dividing family members. For not only do parents and children often end up with different native languages, their different relationships to these languages can have notable social consequences. (Bammer, 1994, p. 100)

Every language is linked to a culture and depends on the concrete context that provides it with meaning and boundaries. "Language determines one's knowledge of the world, of others, and of oneself. It provides a basis of support for one's identity" (Grinberg & Grinberg, 1984, p. 109). To some extent, our language and our way of life are one and the same. When parents and children are fluent in different languages, they may, in fact, be guided by different cultural codes.

Language—the parents' lack of fluency in the new language and the children's lack of fluency in the mother tongue—subverts authority in the family. The power of children is increased because they become "cultural brokers," while the power of parents is decreased because they depend on their children's assistance to survive in the new world. The inordinate amount of power children may acquire because of their language proficiency can be the source of conflicts over authority issues. It also magnifies children's conscious or unconscious fears that their parents are now unable to protect them as they used to. Novena, who was immersed in this situation when she was interviewed, described the difficulties this entailed for her and her parents. Other interviewees referred to similar experiences when describing their adolescence and childhood.

The ease with which one adapts to the new language is determined by a variety of factors, such as the age of migration, individual talent, the degree of similarity between the native language and the new one, and the motivation and opportunity to learn. Emotional factors are of primary importance in this process as well. The mother tongue surrounds the child with protective warmth from the beginning of life. It contributes to the development of a sense of identity even years before the child is actually able to talk.

An immigrant's resistance to language learning may be an expression of a desire for self-preservation. Entering the world of a new language may pose a threat to the individual's sense of identity. Individuals who learn the new language at a fast pace may have less of a stake in preserving another identity. This may be why children learn faster. When confronted by a new language, the immigrant feels excluded. Learning a new language may also generate feelings of guilt at being disloyal to the parents' language. Conversely, learning a new language provides the immigrant with the opportunity to "create a new self." This facilitates working through early conflicts and finding new ways of self-expression that may not have been available in the world of the first language.

> People who learn to use two languages have two symbols for every object. Thus, from an early age, they become emancipated from linguistic symbols—from the concreteness, arbitrariness, and "tyranny" of words—developing analytic abilities. . . to think in terms more . . . independent of the actual word. . . . By contrast, monolinguals may be at a disadvantage. (Portes & Rumbaut, 1996, pp. 200–201)

Polish Australian linguist Anna Wierzbicka (1994) speaks about the difficulty of sorting out awareness of feelings from the interpretation imposed on them by language. According to her research, feelings one reports in different languages through equivalent words often differ in content because of the different context. Normal attitudes toward feelings, emotions, and their verbal and nonverbal expression vary across cultures. She warns us that using English words for analyzing and describing emotions can impose an Anglocentric perspective on our understanding of people's reality. Monolingual speakers of English as well as bilinguals speaking in English are subjected to this influence.

A new language challenges one's self-definitions and the forms of self-expression familiar within one's first language. The women's stories herein illustrate aspects of this process.

As a therapist I came to understand the significance of which language a bilingual client chose for a given subject. This understanding informs my interpretations in this book. Several studies of language choice in therapy with bilinguals illuminate its significance (e.g., Amati-Mehler et al., 1993; Javier, 1989; Krapf, 1955; Marcos, 1976a, 1976b; Rosensky & Gómez, 1983). Psychologist Rafael Javier (1989) described how bilingual individuals mobilize and shift their languages under anxiety-producing conditions. He argued this shifting of languages can be utilized as a coping mechanism. Amati-Mehler and her collaborators (1993) described the enacting of defenses, splittings, and repressions that can occur in psychoanalytic treatment when the patient can speak more than one language. Nevertheless, the impact of language in therapy with bilingual immigrant clients is still not clearly understood; issues of language in therapy have been mostly studied and described from a monolingual perspective.

According to Luis Marcos, a clinician who has studied the impact of language in a bilingual therapy context, when bilinguals are not fully proficient in their second language, they may appear withdrawn. Hence, attention paid to how things are said in therapy may distract attention from what is being said, and this may impair the therapeutic process (1976a). Proficient bilinguals whose languages may be cognitively independent from each other may use this ability as a mechanism for compartmentalizing feelings (Marcos & Alpert, 1976). These mechanisms may render unavailable to the therapeutic process certain areas of the bilingual's intrapsychic world. Marcos and Urcuyo (1979) described the subjective experience of some bilingual individuals who reported a dual sense of self as a consequence of using different languages.

In my clinical practice the importance of language was expressed directly and indirectly. An example of a client's direct intuitive sense of the importance of the first language in therapy came from a college-age Latina woman. She sought me out for therapy specifically because I could speak Spanish. She was fluently bilingual and did not need Spanish to communicate her feelings with sophistication. However, she wanted to have a Spanish-speaking therapist because "My problems are with my family and my family speaks Spanish, so my problems are in Spanish" (Espín, 1994a). Other prospective clients have expressed the same desire and reasoning.

Bilinguals conversing with each other switch from one language to another easily. No significant psychological pattern is apparent in this process. Speakers may choose expressions in the native or second language depending on the relative applicability of the expression to the context. As a bilingual therapist working with bilingual women, I remained alert to their language choice. I did this as any therapist would remain alert to a client's choice of words. As an interviewer of bilingual immigrant women, I tried to remain alert to possible areas of conflict. This frequently concerned sexuality issues that were avoided or expressed by sudden shifts in language. After these experiences, I have come to believe that the choice of language for people who have the option to switch is not simply a matter of arbitrary choice. Rather there appear to be hidden deeper meanings to this selection of which the speaker herself may not be consciously aware.

The interviewees' descriptions of their relation to their languages and to English when speaking about sexuality illustrate some of the twists and complications created by the multilingual experience.

Language and Sexuality

The first language often remains the language of emotions even among immigrants who are fluent in English. The topic of sexuality is an emotional one for most of us. For women—particularly immigrant women—the subject is additionally charged with the many contextual layers within which it develops. Since most of what we know about people's inner feelings comes to us through language, the language chosen to discuss sexuality may determine the accessibility and aware- ness of emotional content (Espín, 1987b; Wierzbicka, 1994).

At best, decoding those affective meanings through the use of another language is problematic. In some instances, the use of English rather than the mother tongue may act as a barrier or resis- tance in dealing with certain components of the psyche. Conversely, the second language can act to facilitate the emergence and discus- sion of certain topics that may be taboo in the native language. Others may refer to the new components of the self acquired through acculturation after English became the primary or most frequently used language. González-Reigosa (1976) has demonstrated that taboo words in the language of origin elicit maximum anxiety. They cause more angst than either taboo words in the second language or indifferent words in the first language. Words that relate to sexuality easily qualify as emotionally charged taboo words.

Thus, speaking in a second language may distance the immigrant woman from important parts of herself. But a second language also may provide a vehicle to express what is inexpressible in the first language—either because the first language does not have the vocab- ulary or because the person censors herself from saying certain taboo things in the first language (Espín, 1984, 1987b, 1995, 1996a, 1996c; Necef, 1994). As we saw in Chapter 3, interviewees stated repeatedly that the second language facilitates ease of communication most when the topic discussed is sexuality. Cultures that have fairly tradi- tional (i.e., conservative) views of female sexuality frequently make it difficult to discuss these issues (Espín, 1984, 1987b; Necef, 1994). If one comes from such a culture, English provides a vehicle for discussing sexual issues that are too embarrassing to discuss with forbidden words in one's first language. Some of the interviewees who came from cultures they defined as "more liberal" than main-stream American culture still preferred to use English in discussions of sexuality. In my therapeutic practice this was particularly signifi-cant for bilingual lesbians. They described their life situation and choices most frequently in English. They tended to avoid equivalent words in their native tongue. Lorena's description of her relationship to her first language vividly illustrates this point.

My therapeutic practice and narrative research lead me to believe that the language in which messages about sexuality are first conveyed and encoded impacts the language chosen to express sexual thoughts, feelings, and ideas. In fact, evidence suggests "memories of personal events are linguistically organized in bilinguals" (Javier et al., 1993, p. 336). In a recent study of autobiographical memory among bilinguals, psychologist Rafael Javier and his collaborators posited that "the nature of bilingual memory is influenced by the kind of linguistic organization the individual develops . . . [and] how and when the two languages are learned will determine the nature of the linguistic orga-nization possible" (Javier et al., 1993, p. 322). Their study suggests there are "differences in the way memories of personal events are organized linguistically in bilinguals [and] . . . that the communica-tion of memories of personal events is qualitatively different in the two languages" (p. 334).

Memories appear to be loaded in favor of the language in which the experience took place. In other words, "the language of the expe-rience may not necessarily be (the bilingual person's) primary language . . . [but rather] the linguistic context in which the verbal interaction occurs" (p. 335). Their findings also suggest that the experience is remembered differently in each language. The fullest expression of the memory combines elements from both languages.

Javier's results have obvious implications for research on bilingual immigrant women's life narratives like those presented herein.

Language and Identity

In addition to the emotional value associated with one's first or second language, language among immigrants signifies degrees of self-esteem. In the United States, bilingualism is popularly associated with inferior social status. Bilingual skills in immigrants are frequently devalued. Schools may inadvertently encourage rejection of parents as "ignorant" people because of their lack of fluency in English. Parents are contrasted with "educated" monolingual teachers. The immigrant child is encouraged to strive for unaccented English at the fastest possible pace. Indeed, language in the United States

> has a meaning that transcends its purely instrumental value as a means of communication. . . . In the United States, the acquisition of nonaccented English and the dropping of foreign languages represent the litmus test of Americanization. (Portes & Rumbaut, 1996, p. 194)

Learning the language of the host society implies learning one's place in the structures of social inequality. The use of the mother tongue is made difficult by these negative connotations. Yet the mother tongue may prove a valuable instrument for reclaiming parts of the self that may have been rejected through the process of acculturation. Thus one's preference to use one language over another is deeply related to identity. But language choice also illuminates other factors such as nationalism, minority status, ethnic pride, cognitive processes encouraged by a particular cultural context, and so on (Edwards, 1985; Espín, 1984, 1987b, 1994a; Hymes, 1961; Necef, 1994). Language choice may also be modulated by the salience of other personal factors affecting cultural identity, as we saw in the case of Cornelia.

Scholarship has indisputably established that language is more than vocabulary and grammar rules. Firsthand accounts from bilingual individuals illustrate the evocative power of one's language usage or choices. Writer Theodor Kallifatides (1992) eloquently described the impact of the Swedish language—versus his native Greek—on his identity, sense of self, and perception of the world. Language profoundly affected his ability to construct metaphors as a writer. For him, "learning a new language is understanding the society that uses it, becoming part of it and somehow surrendering yourself to it" (p. 4), a process that made him feel "a little less Greek" (p. 5).

The meshing of the two languages occurs over time for most immigrants:

> The problem of identity emerges in discussions of language and how to give voice to a multiple heritage. The obvious and yet revolutionary answer is through the use of mixing of the codes that have shaped experience. (Torres, 1991, p. 279)

Most bilinguals do this daily in conversations with each other, which becomes problematic only when they live in two monolingual worlds. Eva Hoffman's (1989) fascinating autobiographical account, already cited, portrays the impact of language on her life as an immigrant. She poignantly describes her split between her Polish-speaking and her English-speaking selves. According to her, she felt like an integrated person only after she narrated the events that "happened to her in Polish" in therapy in English. Her experience personifies how psychotherapy constructs a meaningful story out of disjointed, painful, and contradictory events in one's life.

Interviewees' Use of Language as They Discuss Sexuality

The focus groups and interviews of the main study explored the relationship between different languages and sexual topics. Specifically, questions probed what was permissible to say about sex and in which language one would voice it. Given the proven importance of linguistic categories in narrative studies, particular attention was paid to the language in which the narrative was told by those women whose first language I understood (since this made the conversation possible in either language). Specific attention was paid toward respondents' comfort or discomfort with sexually descriptive terms in their first language. It is possible that when immigrants utilize the two languages in addressing sexuality, this may be a step toward integrating both cultural backgrounds. The exclusive preference of one language over another may compartmentalize the contradictions inherent in being an immigrant.

Most of the women interviewed reported resorting to English when describing their sexuality. Interestingly, while almost all participants prefer to use English to *talk about* sex and sexuality, some respondents preferred their first language *in sexual interactions*. They found words in their first language more sexually arousing. As Maritza stated, it seemed difficult if not impossible to "make love in English."

Two patterns regarding language usage emerged among the participants. In several cases, after the completion of an interview or group session conducted in English, participants said that they could have expressed themselves and answered my questions and comments more easily in their first language. Yet the same participants believed that although they had a larger vocabulary in their first language, it was easier for them to talk about these topics in English. They reported that feelings of shame would have prevented them from addressing these topics in depth in their first language. Marguerite, Hilde, and Ursula exemplify this position. Other participants said that they could not have had this conversation in their first language; they did not know or were unfamiliar with talking about sexuality in their native language. These women had migrated at an early age, usually before or during early adolescence, and had developed their knowledge of sex while immersed in English. They used English more consistently in other spheres of life and felt more comfortable with it. These same women explained that they found it inconceivable to use their first language to talk about adult interactions, including sex and sexuality. Jazmin, Lin, and Mei are examples of this position.

The preference for the second language when addressing issues of sexuality was clearly observable among lesbian immigrants. Lorena in particular demonstrates this pattern. Most of the heterosexual interviewees also preferred the second language when discussing sexuality. Thus it seems a typical pattern for immigrant women regardless of sexual orientation. This preference appears to be fairly stable among the respondents.

These findings are noteworthy because they apparently contradict traditional sociolinguistic theory. Sociolinguistic theorists (e.g., Fishman et al., 1975) argue that bilinguals use their first language for close relationships and intimacy and their second language for business and "the outside world." The first language might be used in the context of love, family, or neighborhood. The second language is used at work or in the classroom, where deep emotions are not at the core of the interaction. Language serves as an instrument that either enhances intimacy (the native tongue) or provides distance in relationships (the second language). Accordingly, the mother tongue should be the language of sexual conversations. However, sexual issues may be the exception to this established sociolinguistic rule.

Turkish Danish scholar Mehmet Necef (1994) contends that the issue is one of clashes in values more than language. If the words learned to discuss sexuality in the first language are "dirty" words, then the native speaker of that language may not be able to describe positive sexual experiences. The second language, then, may become helpful. It provides an acceptable vocabulary to talk about these issues. When a good experience has no name in one language, the bilingual person has the option of resorting to the other language.

Specific characteristics of the first language can also influence the language choice. Sometimes a society and culture lack the language to describe or validate an experience. This is consistent with classic ethnographic linguistic studies that assert that concepts are elaborated in languages depending on the importance of the particular concept to the specific culture. While this is not a linear relationship, the absence or presence of terms in any language is often suggestive of values. It may result from cumulative differences in the selective perceptions and cognitions of linguistic communities over time (Hymes, 1961).

It is not clear if the creative answer that most participants in these studies have developed to address issues of sexuality fits or contradicts the usual bilingual pattern of mixing codes and languages. Many intriguing questions are raised by these data: First, is the immigrant woman's preference for English when discussing sexuality motivated by characteristics of English as a language (i.e., do characteristics of a specific second language offer a vehicle for expression that is unavailable in the first language)? Or does a second language (no matter which one) offer the degree of emotional distance needed to express taboo subjects? If the latter were true, then people whose second language is not English would find it easier also to discuss sexuality in their second language. Because English was the second or third language for those interviewed, it was impossible to assess this possibility, although Aurelia's description of her relationship to the Thai language appears to confirm this point. Second, does the new cultural context—where English is spoken—allow more expression of the woman's feelings? To many immigrants American society seems more sexually permissive behaviorally and verbally than their society of origin. Perhaps the presumed permissiveness of American society encourages and facilitates the expression of these topics in English. This may be true for women who immigrated from traditional societies. Yet this does not explain the preference for English among those women who migrated from more progressive societies (e.g., Germany or Holland, whose less "puritan" attitudes concerning sexuality were reported by Maya, Inge, Ursula, and Hilde). Third, one other possibility may be particularly relevant for those who migrated as children or adolescents. Since they came of age sexually "in English," sexual expression may become inextricably associated with the language. (An analogy exists with professional terminology acquired in a second language.) This scenario would make their preference for English dependent on their learning context rather than on emotional factors, cultural background, or the characteristics of either language. But this alternative does not explain the preference for speaking about sex in English expressed by the interviewees who migrated as adults.

This research reveals that the stronger the cognitive psychological identity development is in one's native language, the greater the comfort when using it in intimate sexual relationships and encounters. However, the discourse about those encounters may continue to benefit from the "opening" provided by a second language. Indeed, the research also reveals how the access to more than one language pushes at the boundaries of what is "sayable" or "tellable." The concomitant effect on the shaping of identity as a consequence of the increased narrative alternatives is also evident.

6 | Mothers, Daughters, and Migration

The process of migration has been metaphorically compared to the human developmental process and its successive stages. Argentinean psychoanalysts Grinberg and Grinberg (1984) suggest that all human development is a migratory process. Through psychological growth individuals move progressively away from their first love objects toward the development of a personal individual identity and sense of self. Most psychodynamic theory considers the mother the primary love object. From this theoretical perspective, the process of migration will be affected and emotionally tinged by the quality of one's relationship with one's mother. But regardless of theoretical orientation, with mother present or absent, migration affects the mother-daughter relationship significantly.

It has become apparent through the interviews that the mother-daughter relationship has been an important mechanism for identity development for these women; they either identify with their mothers or see themselves as very different from them. In either case, examples of the mothers' lives and choices were invoked to explain and justify the daughters' choices. Although this may be a common pattern for all young women, regardless of immigration status, the subjective experience of immigrant daughters is intensified by the marked differences between their life experiences and those of their mothers. If the immigrant woman chooses to identify closely with her mother, she still has to acknowledge the different histories and life stages lived in different countries. If she chooses to differentiate herself as much as possible from her mother, the external circumstances provide her ample opportunity to find dissimilarities in their experiences. Generational differences affect acculturation and differential access to the host culture. Specifically, the daughter's usually faster adjustment to a new culture has an impact on the relationship with her mother. In particular, women who migrate alone during adolescence and early adulthood struggle to redefine and reconstruct their relationships with their mothers and in that process redefine and reconstruct their own identity.

Primary importance was given in these studies to the messages transmitted between mothers and daughters. Messages concerning sexuality and its related issues were emphasized in the main study reported herein. Worldwide, mothers and other older women transmit values to their daughters and other younger women about sexual issues. These messages are rarely conveyed in a structured way (e.g., "Let me teach you about this topic"). In most cultures, messages about womanhood and sexuality are conveyed through half-muttered comments, behavior, example, and—powerfully—through silence. Women of older generations pass along values and beliefs about appropriate gender and sexual behavior by what they say about men and other women, and by teaching by example what is allowed or forbidden in the culture of origin. These include ideas about what "good" women should and should not do according to the norms of the particular culture. The messages frequently include other issues such as women's reproductive health, pregnancy and menstruation, heterosexual intercourse and male-female relationships, and so forth. These messages continue to be powerful injunctions for first-, second-, and even third-generation immigrant women and have profound psychological and health consequences. All the interviewees spoke about the impact of these conversations or silences on their lives. What women learn to believe about their position in relation to men, for example, has vital implications for their well-being.

Examples include the prevention of AIDS and other sexually transmitted diseases, prevention of domestic violence and adolescent pregnancy, use of contraceptives and abortion decisions, and so on (Marin et al., 1992; Marin et al., 1993).

The transmission of these ideas as well as their content is not unproblematic. Prescriptive sexual ideology for women in immigrant communities manifests itself through protective behaviors toward daughters and through contradictory messages that may become difficult to disentangle.

As philosopher Uma Narayan (1997) states,

> in all cultures mothers give all sorts of contradictory messages, encouraging their daughters to be confident, impudent, and self-assertive, even as they attempt to instill conformity, decorum, and silence, seemingly oblivious to these contradictions. (p. 8)

Sometimes mothers become "critical of the effects of the very things they encourage" (Narayan, 1997, p. 8) because they seem unaware that they are raising their daughters with contradictory messages.

> They give voice to the hardships and difficulties of being a woman that have marked their lives, teaching us the limitations and miseries of the routine fates that await us as women, while also resisting our attempts to deviate from these cultural scripts. (Narayan, 1997, p. 8)

In other words, "the same mothers who complained about their silencing, enjoined [their] daughters to silence . . . [without awareness] that the shape [their] 'silence' took is in part what incited [the daughter] to speech" (Narayan, 1997, p. 8).

The focus groups and individual interviews explored what mothers as transmitters of cultural norms tell (or don't tell) their daughters about what they should (or should not) do as women. Conversations in the groups and individual interviews focused on generational differences among women about gender-role expectations and sexual behavior. In the interviews, younger women talked about their perceptions of their mothers' expression of and comfort with sexuality. Interviewees who were mothers articulated their concerns with their daughters' sexuality and their desire to do better than their own mothers.

Many of the women interviewed had internalized their mothers' fears and self-doubts. Often these were transmitted as silences on the subject of sex. Mothers were frequently perceived as unable to accept their own sexuality, let alone their daughters'. Some, like Leticia, actively feared transmitting her mothers' shame and guilt concerning sexuality to her daughter.

In an earlier study of mother-daughter separation due to migration (Espín et al., 1990), my collaborators and I argued that migration inevitably complicated the relationship. The women in this study were asked to specifically focus on their relationships with their mothers before and after migration. Their responses were varied. Their relationships with their mothers before migration ranged from tense and distant to extremely close. Despite quality differences within these dyads prior to migration, most participants emphasized the migration's positive effects on their bond with their mothers, while acknowledging some negative experiences of the migration itself.

Some of the changes on the mother-daughter dyad and on the daughter's psychological development were attributed to the acculturation process. The primary transformations of the relationship between daughters and mothers were attributed to the daughter's new experiences. As she gained understanding of a new culture and way of life not shared by the mother this may have caused friction between them. However, some women, like Violeta, felt these changes improved their relationships with their mothers; they related to each other as two adult women for the first time. Others, like Colleen and Annette, felt that the separation made them miss an opportunity for closeness with their mothers that they could not recover. A few, like Nora, believed that physical distance from their mothers during adolescence or early adulthood did not alter their relationship substantially.

Some examples about the relationship with their mothers provided by interviewees are significant in the graphic description of the new world opened to the daughter from whom the mother is absent. Roya's description of her relationship with her mother exemplifies this situation. Others, like Violeta and Annette, described vividly the new ways of relating that have evolved during the years of geographical distance.

Not surprisingly, the interviewees' relationships with their fathers were less affected by the migration. This was particularly evident in the cases of women who migrated alone during adolescence or young adulthood. They were less affected leaving their fathers behind. It is unclear if this was due to a less intense or less complicated relationship or because they had expected less emotional support from them than from their mothers.

Because women are expected to preserve culture and traditions, immigrant women who are mothers are expected to be the carriers of culture for their children in the new country. They are also made responsible for raising children capable of functioning competently in both cultural worlds. This can become burdensome for the mother, who herself may be overwhelmed with her own adjustment difficulties. It also may present unique challenges for women whose daughters come out as lesbians before or after the migration.

The mothers of the lesbian immigrants interviewed—many of them also immigrants—displayed a continuum of reactions to their daughters' lesbianism. Some, like Maritza's and Violeta's mothers, showed an unexpected supportive reaction, even though they may have not approved fully of their daughters' choices. Others, like Cindy's mother, demanded and expected their daughters' secrecy in front of all other relatives and never referred to their daughters' lesbianism after the initial revelation. In these cases, the mantle of silence acted as an active rejection of the daughter's life. In a few cases such as Eva, Maya, and Ursula, their lesbianism does not seem to have been an issue for their mothers. These three mothers, like Maritza's mother, were not immigrants. Violeta's and Cindy's mothers had immigrated with their families. Thus, mothers' immigration status and cultural background did not appear to have any relationship to their acceptance of daughters' lesbianism. In any case, the transformations of daughters' sexuality and sexual identities—in addition to their own—had to be confronted by the mothers. Cecilia is an interesting and unique case among the interviewees because she is both a mother and a lesbian. In her case, the acceptance had to come from her children, who were already adults when she came out and who had been born in the United States after her migration. Because she had migrated many years before her coming out these processes were not intertwined for her as for other interviewees.

Angelika Bammer (1994) aptly asserts "the need for a model of family that recognizes cultural displacement as a central factor shaping human development and social reality in our century" (p. 102). She believes that "to the extent that the family constitutes a critical nexus in the realms of the psychological and the social/political, such a model is all the more necessary" (p. 103). This new model of family should incorporate the conflicts between motherhood and breadwinner roles that become much more dramatic for women who are expected to mother in traditional ways in the midst of cultural dislocation. Women who have been raised to be self-denying and self-sacrificing mothers may lose themselves—and their physical and mental health—in this situation.

"Among today's immigrants, women with female kin or with close friends . . . more often avoid illness, depression, and mental illness than those who feel isolated from other women" (Gabaccia, 1994, p. 121). Feminist writer Marianne Hirsch, who immigrated during her adolescence, writes that her "friendship [with other women] provided a form of displacement and resistance: to cultural assimilation as well as to femininity" (1994, p. 88). Ironically, the multiplicity of roles demanded of mothers by the new society frequently interferes with the possibility of developing and maintaining the very friendship relationships that could preserve sanity in the middle of chaos.

The conflicting and strenuous demands placed on mothers do not escape the daughters' awareness. Their loyalty and respect for "their culture" is tainted by the awareness that there is little justice or happiness for their mothers in that context (Narayan, 1997). The impetus to "become American" is mixed with this awareness. However, as they learn more about the realities of women's lives in American society, they learn that sexism is also alive and well in the United States. It is therefore not surprising that for some young immigrant women or U.S.-born daughters of immigrants, feminist understandings provide a context in which to manage the contradictions of their mothers' lives as well as their own. Marianne Hirsch writes that "things really [came] together when [she was] able to incorporate female/feminist bonding into [her] work as well as [her] life" (1994, p. 86). Violeta and other study participants described similar experiences in their interviews.

Mothers whose daughters have migrated alone while the rest of the family remains in the home country also experience specific stresses. They may be blamed for the daughter's migration if it contradicts cultural norms, or they may be expected to pressure their daughters to migrate if it seems beneficial for the family (for example, if it is expected that the daughter will send money consistently to the family) or if the daughter's migration fulfills other cultural dictums, such as migrating to join a new and unknown husband for an arranged marriage. In some cases, mothers encourage their daughters to migrate to escape political conflicts or economic despair, as in the cases of Annette, Mina, and Colleen. These are some of the reasons why even when the decision to migrate is apparently the woman's (mother or daughter) it may not be synonymous with self-determination.

In reality, mother-daughter relationships are deeply embedded in a patriarchal context. This is true in non-Western traditional societies as well as in Western countries. Mothers and daughters—as females—have minimal control on this context. Mothering exists in and is modified by the patriarchal expectations of motherhood in all cultures in the world. Mothering occurs within specific social and historical contexts. It is constructed by those forces. We cannot fully understand the process of women's migration until we interpret patriarchy's effect on it and on the mother-daughter relationship. Any future study of the process of migration and its impact on women's lives needs to analyze the impact of patriarchal cultural norms on the mother-daughter relationship and its significance to the migration experience for both the mother and the daughter.

The Experience
of Lesbian Immigrants

7

While lesbians and gay men obviously exist among immigrants, many immigrant communities prefer to believe otherwise. Some posit that homosexuality is just an evil of modern societies, acquired by contagion or through the bad influences of the new society (e.g., Espín, 1987a; Tremble, Schneider, & Appathurai, 1989). They prefer to believe that homosexuality is either nonexistent in their communities or that it could be eradicated were it not for the bad influence of acculturation. My research recognizes that both lesbians and heterosexual women cross geographical and psychological borders.

Difficulties prevail in obtaining adequate statistics on lesbian populations among immigrants and refugees. Demographic studies suggest that the composition of the gay and lesbian population in North America is very much like the entire population in terms of ethnic, racial, and national origin background (Tremble, Schneider, & Appathurai, 1989). Most likely, several million lesbians and gay men are among the immigrant population in the United States. The numbers are even higher if we factor immigrants and refugees worldwide.

There are emotional and practical difficulties of migration for lesbians as for other immigrants. These are compounded by the difficulties created by prevalent stereotyped conceptions of womanhood and sexuality in both the home and host cultures, familial and societal rejection of their sexual identity, and legal restrictions on their immigration. Still, the new environment may open up possibilities hitherto unavailable in the country of birth. Paramount among these is the possibility of living a lesbian life.

The immigrant lesbian acculturates to the new society as an immigrant as well as to the particular lesbian culture in which she is situated. Thus lesbians who are immigrants or refugees share experiences with heterosexual women from their particular immigrant community as well as with lesbians in the host culture. They also share some experiences with gay males who are immigrants or refugees. Their political, religious, and social affiliations with their respective immigrant communities and the lesbian community vary greatly. In different degrees, both contexts provide a sense of identification in the host country.

As discussed, immigrant communities intently preserve cultural traditions in the face of massive cultural transformation. The presence of lesbians in their midst is particularly difficult to acknowledge. They prefer to see lesbianism as one of the dangers of the host society. Their communities' expectations create emotional pressures on lesbian immigrants.

Like the immigrant community, which is often hostile, the United States does not provide a warm welcome for lesbians and gay men. Yet despite the historically negative reception or outright rejection through United States immigration laws, most lesbians and gay men still consider immigration to the United States a positive alternative to the harsher persecution they may confront in their homeland.

Legislation concerning the immigration of lesbians and gay men into the United States has been mostly restrictive.[1] The Immigration Act of 1917 excluded "persons of constitutional psychopathic inferiority." In 1952 the Immigration and Nationality Act (INA) reworded its exclusions: "Aliens afflicted with psychopathic personality, epilepsy or a mental defect" were not allowed to enter the United States. The legislative history of these acts shows that this language was broad enough to exclude "homosexuals and sex perverts" (Foss,

1994, p. 446). The 1952 INA was adopted in a climate of national paranoia. Homosexuality was associated with communism not only in the popular mind but by the government as well. Ironically, the Communist Party, like mainstream culture, rejected homosexuals as well (Foss, 1994, pp. 449–450).

These laws started changing in 1979. As a consequence of the American Psychiatric Association's 1973 declaration that homosexuality per se does not constitute mental illness, the surgeon general announced that the Public Health Service, working under the Immigration and Naturalization Service (INS), would no longer exclude aliens suspected of homosexuality. (The INS is the federal agency charged with processing immigrants for admission and, later, for citizenship.)

In 1980 the same federal agency adopted new procedures devoid of questions about sexual orientation. However, a voluntary admission of homosexuality or a third-party disclosure was still used to exclude an alien. Finally, the Immigration Act of 1990 abandoned these provisions. Since then, immigrants have the right to enter openly as lesbians. Technically, those admitted before 1990 can still be deported, since they were admitted when the exclusion was still in effect (Foss, 1994, p. 462).

In the middle 1990s the courts started considering persecution based on sexual orientation as cause for political asylum. Thus refugee status was granted on the basis of sexual orientation (Park, 1995). Historically, this is unprecedented. Two recent cases followed a 1994 directive to the INS from Attorney General Janet Reno. Both held that lesbians and gay men can receive protection under U.S. asylum policy. They can be considered members of a persecuted social group eligible for refugee status under the law (Park, 1995, p. 1120). (So far, the precedent-setting legal cases have involved gay men.) Despite Reno's directives, problems still exist. Proving persecution will be harder for closeted lesbians and gays, while open homosexuals will encounter less difficulty demonstrating that they are closely affiliated and share similar interests with other members of the persecuted group. This is an essential condition that the immigrant must demonstrate in order to justify the need for asylum.

The Lesbian and Gay Immigration Rights Task Force, a nonprofit organization advocating the reform of discriminatory immigration laws in the United States that affect lesbians and gay men, is still concerned with several issues despite these recent positive changes. For example, the Immigration and Nationality Act permits the immigration of a foreign spouse, yet lesbians and gays are still prevented from bringing foreign partners to the United States because same-sex marriages are still not legal here. (And even if same-sex marriage is legalized, it probably will take years of legal battles to persuade the INS to recognize these marriages for immigration purposes.)

Many lesbians and gay men have experienced persecution in their homelands. But even in cases where active persecution did not occur, the lesbians interviewed felt more at ease away from their countries and families. For example, Maritza sought escape from societal and familial constraints on her lesbianism. Maya, although not particularly constricted by Dutch society, also found new freedom as a lesbian in North America. In these two cases at least, their lesbianism inspired their migration. For others like Olga and Lorena, the migration provided the space and permission to come out at a later date.

Lesbianism is closely connected with sexual behavior and identity, although it is not only about sex. As discussed in Chapter 4, sexuality, a universal component of human experience, is embodied and expressed in various ways. Even the definition of what is sexual changes among cultures. These cultural constructs are intertwined with lesbians' expression of their sexuality. As lesbian communities also vary across countries and even regionally within the same country, many women who identified as lesbian before the migration have to learn to be lesbian in their new cultural context. If a lesbian is from a non-European background, she also faces acculturation as a (so-called) minority person. Many of these women have experienced discrimination because of their sexuality before the migration, and some experience discrimination based on sexual orientation combined with ethnic discrimination after the migration. As I found when researching the adjustment of immigrant lesbians in the 1980s:

> Coming out to self and others in the context of a sexist and heterosexist American society is compounded by coming out in the context of what is usually a sexist and heterosexist [culture of origin] immersed in racist society. (Espín, 1987a, p. 35)

Lesbians who "come out" as adolescents present unique challenges to immigrant communities. As the authors of a study on Canadian youth remind us,

> Every adolescent, regardless of ethnic affiliation, must resolve a number of issues as part of the coming-out process. These include: (a) deciding whether or not to disclose to the family, (b) finding a niche among gay and lesbian peers, and (c) reconciling sexual orientation with other aspects of identity. For the child of immigrant parents, the coming-out process takes place against the backdrop of ethnic traditions, values, and social networks. . . . The rift that occurs between parent and child over sexual orientation is set in the context of an existing conflict as the child pulls away from the Old World culture to espouse the North American way of life. (Tremble, Schneider, & Appathurai, 1989, p. 255)

These researchers argue that, paradoxically, these values also provide the pathway to reconciliation between homosexual children and parents. Strong familial love and family ties will withstand these stressers. Ultimately, the lesbian or gay child is embraced (Tremble, Schneider, & Appathurai, 1989).

Whether adolescent or adult, lesbian immigrants face specific burdens concerning life decisions. Disclosure of sexual orientation affects them as individuals, and it affects the community's perception of itself as well. Coming out may jeopardize family ties, as well as their much-needed contributions to their community. For example, many lesbian immigrants are single and self-supporting and take advantage of employment and educational opportunities in the United States (Espín, 1987a). They are frequently involved in services and advocacy for their communities. Simultaneously, they feel constrained in their service to their community for fear of being "discovered" and rejected (Espín, 1987a, 1996c). It is not unusual to encounter leaders in immigrant communities who consider themselves radical and committed to civil rights, but who remain extremely traditional when it comes to gay and lesbian civil rights.

The typical immigrant's ruminations about "what could have been" are magnified by lesbians' perspectives on past events seen in a new light after coming out. Some lesbians become preoccupied with the relationship between childhood events and their realization of their lesbianism. To this, the immigrant lesbian adds the question: Would I have become a lesbian if I had not emigrated?

The interviews reveal lesbians' comfort with descriptive terms about lesbianism in their first and second language. For lesbians, the choice of language when describing sexuality may feel more poignant than for heterosexual women because their sexual behavior may be more associated with taboo words. Lorena's description of her difficulties speaking about lesbianism in her native language as well as Cindy's lack of vocabulary in hers illustrate some of the issues language usage and biligualism evoke for lesbian immigrants.

Most of the lesbians interviewed described a broader cultural openness regarding lesbianism in the United States than in their home country, which created a conflict of loyalties. Their home cultures provided comfort and stability through their families and cultural traditions yet limited their lesbian lives. This was the case for almost all of them. For example, both Maritza and Olga are out to their families. Although there is no particular conflict with their family members concerning their lesbianism, their parents and siblings wish they lived a heterosexual life. Lorena and Cindy, neither of whom is fully out to their families, find that expressing their sexuality in their culture of origin is even more conflictual.

The developmental stage each lesbian was in at the time of migration and coming out dramatically modified their individual experiences. Those who migrated after adolescence were less conflicted about their lesbianism. This may be because their identities were somewhat solid before migration. Similarly, for those who migrated at a later developmental stage the process was less disruptive when the coming out process occurred after the migration.

The contradictions and paradoxes of the processes of acculturation and coming out tend to follow a predictable pattern. Initially, self-definition is not conscious, and awareness of ethnicity and sexual orientation progresses as growth and development continue. They tend to pass through a period in which they internalize society's views of ethnic groups and sexual orientation. Later, some become active in political and community activities and may go through a militant phase in which they come to understand the nature of racism, heterosexism, and oppression more deeply. Eventually, if identity development proceeds positively, they are able to appreciate as well as critically analyze their cultural heritage, American society, and the lesbian communities in which they are immersed.

The development of this internal process of self-knowledge and adjustment affects lesbian immigrants' life choices and adds depth to the process of identity formation (Espín, 1987a). The varied scope of their experiences illustrates vividly the notion that "identity is not one thing for any individual; rather, each individual is both located in, and opts for, a number of differing and, at times, conflictual, identities, depending on the social, political, economic and ideological aspects of their situation" (Bhavnani & Phoenix, 1994, p. 9).

The transitions implied in the migratory process can provide additional insights in the process of coming out for all lesbians, including those who are not immigrants. They are a metaphor for the crossing of borders and boundaries that all lesbians confront when refusing to continue living in old ways. As previously discussed, the immigrant's acculturation into a new society is first and foremost a process of disassembling and reassembling social networks (Rogler, 1994). The process of coming out also involves a disassembling and reassembling of one's life and social networks regardless of immigration status. In other words, examination of the discontinuities induced by migration also sheds light on the discontinuities induced by the coming out process for all lesbians. This understanding has significance for learning how other social groups negotiate lesbian identity and the coming out process, and can expand our outlook on the alternatives available to all lesbians (Espín, 1996c).

Note

1. This section on legislation is closely modeled after my entry, entitled "Immigration," which appears in B. Zimmerman (Ed.). (1999). *The encyclopedia of lesbian histories and cultures*. New York: Garland.

8 | Final Thoughts

I have tried in this book to convey something of what the process of migration into another country means for women. I began by outlining the parameters of the migration experience from the perspective of women. I argued that the production of psychological knowledge has been constrained by the adherence to quantitative methods and the emphasis on measurable behavior that do not provide space for the subjective. I described the value of personal narrative in capturing some elements of human experience and explained my rationale for using stories as the source of data on women's experience of migration. I see the possibilities of this methodology and devote a large portion of this book to the stories of the women interviewed. The richness of these data speaks for itself. I ground my perspectives on those stories and on my theoretical understanding of their meaning. My focus has been on psychological aspects of women's experience of migration, with a particular emphasis on sexuality and gender roles. No account of the psychological meaning of the experience of migration is final, but some key themes keep recurring in my thoughts as well as in the pages of this book.

The multiple migrations that characterize our world are rooted in vast historical and political processes. These have resulted in the creation of refugee populations and the lure of economic opportunities for many people. This book has been informed by the view that thinking psychologically should incorporate the effects of the social world and historical dislocations on the intrapsychic life of individuals. My intention was not to create a sense of grand narrative but rather to present a window into the individual life narratives developed by women who have been immersed in the transformations brought about by migration.

Narratives have a unique appeal. They provided a unique vehicle for my commitment to enable these women to be heard. Incorporating their own meaning-making efforts into my understanding of their experiences was an essential part of this project. This carried with it the additional task of interpreting the experiences of people who were engaged in the process of interpreting themselves. Because I have shared similar life experiences with these women, I was both glad to serve as their mouthpiece and wary about the dangers of representing them. No matter how similar those experiences, the researcher and the researched may have very different ideas about "who we are," and no matter how strong the similarities, vast differences in experience were also present. Differences between my experience and my interviewees' as well as differences among the interviewees themselves originate in the dissimilar countries of birth, ages at migration, historical period when the migration took place, circumstances surrounding migration, and the ultimate consequences of the process for each individual life. Each one of these women carried into the interview the history of all these events intertwined with her personal history.

Despite those differences, several behavioral patterns became clear through the interviews. Most of the women revised their social and gender role expectations as a consequence of their migration. They worked hard at renegotiating gender roles with both the traditions of their home country and the expectations of the host culture. Their experiences illustrate the simultaneous process of acculturation and identity formation. Adult interviewees who had migrated during adolescence had dealt with this developmental task long before the interview. The younger ones were still questioning where they belong and who they would become; they were in the midst of this process at the time of the interview. The older ones both reminisce and ponder what life would have been like under different circumstances. In general, their adaptations appear to be successful despite differences in individual histories and personalities and in their choice of individual paths.

In most cases, the interviewees' descriptions of their family life confirm that

> patriarchal gender relations undergo continual renegotiation as women and men rebuild their families in the United States. Gender is reconstructed in different ways, guided by the limits imposed by particular contexts and patterns of migration, but family and community relations exhibit a general shift in the direction of gender egalitarianism. . . . These changes do not occur in ways that conform to any formulaic linear stages. They happen unevenly, and often result in contradictory combinations of everyday practices. (Hondagneu-Sotelo, 1994, p. 193)

The loss involved in migration was addressed repeatedly by many of the interviewees. They also countered forcefully the perception of losses with the argument that the experience of migration had enriched them and given them choices, options, and fluency in a repertoire of languages, modes of thought, and social networks. The opportunities in work, education, and routines of life provided by the migration had a special significance for these women. Regardless of differences in their birth countries concerning the roles of women, they all benefited from the liberating effect of being outsiders.

Nevertheless, migration also carries with it the possibility of limiting women's private spheres of influence and their moral authority within traditional cultural contexts. Traditional patriarchal contexts have always provided women with the opportunity to carve separate—if inferior—spaces. The cultural transformations brought about by migration upset these spaces without yet giving women full access to equal power in the public sphere. For immigrant daughters, it may become difficult to invest the mother with positive images and characteristics when migration has limited her sphere of influence even further. The mother, increasingly expected to fulfill the duties of enforcing patriarchal rules vis à vis her daughter, may become embittered by her own lack of opportunity. Because the father benefits from the power of patriarchy, he may become more attractive to the daughter as a role model. Migration might subvert this structure when the father loses power as a consequence of a lowered status in the world because of his condition as an immigrant. A father whose options have also become more limited because of language and other difficulties created by migration presents a problematic alternative for his children. If this situation is coupled with the mother's increased independence and participation in the public sphere, it is possible that her status increases in the eyes of her daughter. But patriarchal traditions that interpret women's participation in the public sphere in negative terms may conspire against this possibility.

The life stage and age at the time of migration seemed to have played a significant role in immigrant experience. This connection between age and the impact of a life event is almost self-evident. It confirms psychologist Abigail Stewart's "assumption that one important factor in the attachment of individual meaning to social events is an individual's age, because of the connection between age and stage of psychological development" (1994, p. 231).

Indeed, most conflicts were described by those who migrated during adolescence. This is understandable because of the multiple tasks required of young women immigrants. As a young immigrant woman constructs her identity in a new country, she simultaneously develops a sexual identity. Numerous theorists have acknowledged the important role of sexuality in identity development. The inherent connection between discourses on sexuality and sources of power in a cultural context may result in split identities for young women immigrants. Religious and cultural injunctions may further limit the young woman's decision making. Nevertheless, many young immigrant women successfully negotiate a place for themselves despite these injunctions and limitations and struggle to find their own sexual expression. Young women from racialized groups may confront additional conflicts concerning their sexuality and body image. They have to find a balance between the imposed hyper-sexualization of immigrant women as exotic and the hyper-purity expected of them by their families and communities.

The women who had migrated as children seemed to have adapted faster and easier. However, children whose lives have been affected by major social historical events may be affected in their broad values and expectations about the world at a deeper psychological level. "Children's experience of social historical events is, of course, filtered through their experiences in their own families" (Stewart, 1994, p. 232). Because the migration altered the course of their psychological and material lives early in life, interviewees who had migrated at a very early age were less able to image who and what they could have been without the impact of the migration.

Those who migrated after adolescence appear to be less conflicted. This is due in part to their already somewhat solid identities before undergoing the extra tasks involved in the migration. This is clearly true for lesbian interviewees. Even when the coming out, with its attendant identity changes, had occurred after the migration, the process seemed to have been less disrupting for those who migrated at a later age.

Many of the interviewees described their early sexual experiences and desires—both heterosexual and lesbian—as troubling and fraught with secrecy and ignorance. Others managed to find their own ways and happiness despite their confusion and the struggles and opposition of families.

The issue of language and its impact on identity was also central to the interviews. The ambivalence many interviewees expressed toward one or more of the languages they spoke and toward bilingualism itself was paramount in their experience. Here also, age modified the experience, because it influenced the ability to speak unaccented English versus the ability to fully inhabit the world of their first language. As discussed in Chapter 5, it may be the case that people who speak more than one language are able to defend from and withhold the expression of deep emotion by switching between languages. What then happens for women in intimate relationships with individuals who do not speak their same languages? Many of the women interviewed were interracially or interculturally married. Others, although not married, were in similar situations in heterosexual or lesbian relationships. Do these women become truly intimate and vulnerable in these relationships? Are these relationships a manifestation of healthy transformations or are they a form of escaping intimacy and vulnerability? Is it possible that a deep and significant relationship may develop despite these barriers? Regardless of their deep desires to connect with their partners, are they able to do so? Or are the splits in identity created by language differences an impediment to the success of these relationships? Perhaps, particularly concerning sexuality, nonverbal communication creates the bridge to cross the language divide.

Finally, I would like to assert that increased understanding about beliefs concerning sexuality and gender-related issues among immigrant populations has vital implications for public policy in areas such as prevention of sexually transmitted diseases (including AIDS prevention), unwanted teenage pregnancy, family violence, and similar social problems and health issues (Marín et al., 1992; Marín et al., 1993). Although I would not want to make unwarranted claims, it is possible that information derived from these studies could be used for the development of educational programs. Perhaps these stories could assure families about the eventual success of the painful process of adaptation to American society. They could serve to inform immigrant adolescents and their families about controversial topics and dispel cultural myths while taking into consideration immigrants' own cultural values. This could minimize miscommunication across generations and cultures.

Ultimately, the question faced by this book is who "owns" women's sexuality and lives. Modern ideas about women's right to sexual pleasure and to making free choices concerning their lives have not entirely replaced more traditional ideas about gender obligations and differences in rights. These questions are alive in all societies. Yet they become more poignant and dramatic in the context of traditional groups trying to acculturate in a new context that is itself in transition concerning the role of women. Perhaps participation in these studies and the transformational stories created in these interviews allowed participants to get in touch with their own sexuality and their own erotic power. I hope that these studies contributed to awareness and integration of experiences for the participants as they contribute to others' increased understanding of women's experiences of crossing geographical and emotional boundaries.

Appendix A
Interview Guide: Study of Immigrant Women's Sexuality

This interview is about your life as an immigrant and about the process of adjustment to the U.S. (and/or any other country where you have been an immigrant). I am particularly interested in how this adjustment process has influenced your life as a woman, your understanding of gender roles, and your sexuality/sexual identity (understanding this term in a broad way, to refer not only or specifically to sexual behavior or feelings). For example I am interested in how you learned about menstruation and from whom, what messages you received as a child about the meaning of being female, and what expectations about your behavior in relation to men and other women were conveyed to you in your culture of origin and first language versus those that you learned from the United States mainstream culture and in English. I am also very interested in mother/daughter conversations or silences about these topics and about the impact of those conversations or silences on who you are and how you behave. When interviewing lesbian women, I am particularly interested in how the "coming out" process affected or was affected by the immigration and subsequent acculturation into U.S. society.

This interview is more like an informal conversation in which you say as much or as little about yourself and your life and experiences as you would like. Although the general focus of the interview is sexuality and gender roles, I make every effort to make you feel comfortable and not ask embarrassing questions. PLEASE REMEMBER THAT YOU DO NOT HAVE TO ANSWER ANY QUESTION YOU DO NOT WANT TO ANSWER. If at any point you do not want to answer a question, just say so and we will change the topic. If you want to go deeper into and/or expand on any topic, please feel free to do so. I am here to listen and learn from what you want to tell me about your life concerning these topics.

The interview could be carried out individually or in a group that will focus and interact on the topics of these questions:

Tell me briefly the story of your migration: i.e., leaving your country (why? under what circumstances? at what age? who decided it? what was the process of leaving?); arriving in the U.S. (how old? how did it feel to be here? who came with you? what were the easiest and most difficult aspects of adjusting to life in the U.S.?). Is there anything in your migration story that you believe is particularly unique or important?

What was your family's configuration before migration? Did it change after the migration? If so, how? How did these changes affect you? the structure of your family? What was your family's socioeconomic class in your home country? Did this change in the U.S.? Were you closer to some member of your family than others?

Have there been any changes in your clothing style since you came to the U.S.? Do you dress now as you would dress in your home country? If not, what are the differences? Why the changes? When did you make them?

What did your mother tell you (or did not tell you) about being a woman? menstruation? relating to men? violence in relationships? marriage? having children? being a mother? heterosexual behavior? lesbianism and bisexuality?

Did you have conversations about these topics with anybody else? other adults in your family? at school? older siblings? peers? When and in which country did these conversations happen? at what point in your life?

What language did she/you/they use for these conversations? What language do you prefer to use when talking about these topics or anything else related to sex? What language do you prefer to use when talking about other topics? What language do you prefer to use during sexual encounters/intercourse?

Have most of your sexual partners been members of your same culture or not? If not, what has been/is their background? If you are presently married or in a relationship, what is this person's ethnic/racial background? Is there any relationship between this person's background and your experiences as a woman in your culture of origin? your experiences as an immigrant?

Do you think being an immigrant has made any difference in your life? If so, how? What kind of woman do you think you would have been had you not migrated? How is that the same or different from what you believe you would have been had you stayed in your home country? How would you describe the woman you have come to be? Does migration have anything to do with who you are as a woman now?

Are the messages about sexuality/gender roles/womanhood that you received from your home culture different from those you received from "mainstream" U.S. society? If yes, have these differences been conflictual for you in any way? If so, how? Have you experienced any distress because of the differences in these messages? Can you say more about this?

Do you feel you are comfortable with your sexuality? with being a woman? with being an immigrant? with being from your country of origin? with your race? If yes or if no, can you say more about this? Do you believe being a woman has made it easier or more difficult for you as an immigrant? easier or more difficult to be a person of your race?

Have you ever been abused, sexually or otherwise, or been sexually assaulted? If yes, did this happen in your family or with others? Please say as much or as little about this as you are comfortable with. Have you discussed this with anyone else? Please say more if you can about the conditions of your talking about the above or anything else you think relevant.

For lesbians: Did you "come out" before or after migration? Are "coming out" and migration "connected" for you in any way? Are you out to your family? other people in your country? friends from your country/culture here in the U.S.? Are you more comfortable among lesbian/gays even if not from your culture/country or with people from your culture/country even if they are not gay? Do you think your lesbianism has been affected by the migration in any way? If so, how? Do you think you would have been (or were you already) equally "out" in your country than what you are now in the U.S.? Is it easier or more difficult to talk about lesbianism in English or in your first language?

Is there anything else you would like to say about these topics? about the interview itself?

Thank you very much for your time and trust.

Let me know if you have a preference for any particular pseudonym. Please feel free to contact me in the future if you have any thoughts about this interview.

THANKS AGAIN!

References

Accad, E. (1991). Sexuality and sexual politics: Conflicts and contradictions for contemporary women in the Middle East. In C. T. Mohanty, A. Russo, & L. Torres (Eds.), *Third World women and the politics of feminism* (pp. 237–250). Bloomington, IN: Indiana University Press.

Allport, G. (1942). *The use of personal documents in psychological science*. New York: Social Science Research Council.

Amati-Mehler, J., Argentieri, S., & Conestri, J. (1993). *The Babel of the unconscious: Mother tongue and foreign languages in the psychoanalytic dimension*. Madison, CT: International University Press.

Andizian, S., Catani, M., Cicourel, A., Dittmar, N., Harper, D., Kudat, A., Morokvasic, M., Oriol, M., Parris, R. G., Streiff, J., & Setland, C. (1983). *Vivir entre dos culturas*. Paris: Serbal/UNESCO.

Aron, A. (1992). "Testimonio," a bridge between psychotherapy and sociotherapy. In E. Cole, O. M. Espín, & E. Rothblum (Eds.), *Shattered societies, shattered lives: Refugee women and their mental health* (pp. 173–189). New York: Haworth Press.

Arrendondo-Dowd, P. (1981). Personal loss and grief as a result of immigration. *Personnel and Guidance Journal, 59*, 376–378.

Bakan, D. (1996). Some reflections about narrative research and hurt and harm. In R. Josselson (Ed.), *The narrative study of lives* (Vol. 4, pp. 3–21). Thousand Oaks, CA: Sage.

Bammer, A. (1994). Mother tongues and other strangers: Writing "family" across cultural divides. In A. Bammer (Ed.), *Displacements: Cultural identities in question* (pp. 90–109). Bloomington: Indiana University Press.

Bandura, A. (1982). The psychology of chance encounters and life paths. *American Psychologist, 37*(7), 747–755.

Bar-Yam, A. (1983). *Immigration and adolescence.* Unpublished manuscript. Boston University.

Basch, C. E. (1987). Focus group interview: An underutilized research technique for improving theory and practice in health education. *Health Education Quarterly, 14*, 411–448.

Berry, J. W., & Annis, R. C. (1974). Acculturative stress: The role of ecology culture and differentiation. *Journal of Cross-Cultural Psychology, 5*, 382–405.

Bhavnani, K-K., & Haraway, D. (1994). Shifting the subject: A conversation between Kum-Kum Bhavnani and Donna Haraway, 12 April, 1993, Santa Cruz, California. *Feminism & Psychology, 4*(1), 19–39.

Bhavnani, K-K., & Phoenix, A. (1994). Editorial introduction. Shifting identities Shifting racism. *Feminism & Psychology, 4*(1), 5–18.

Bonierbale, M., Gensollen, J., & Pin, M. (1981). La femme immigrée et la sexualité. *Psychologie Médicale, 13* (11), 1785–1788. [The immigrant woman and sexuality.]

Boszormenyi-Nagy, I., & Spark, C. M. (1973). *Invisible loyalties: Reciprocity in intergenerational family therapy.* New York: Harper & Row.

Braidotti, R. (1994). *Nomadic subjects.* New York: Columbia University Press.

Brettell, C. B., & Sargent, C. F. (Eds.). (1993). *Gender in cross- cultural perspective.* Englewood Cliffs, NJ: Prentice-Hall.

Caplan, P. (1987). *The cultural construction of sexuality.* New York: Routledge.

Cienfuegos, A. I., & Monelli, C. (1983). The testimony of political repression as a therapeutic instrument. *American Journal of Orthopsychiatry, 53*, 43–51.

Cole, E., Espín, O. M., & Rothblum, E. (Eds.). (1992). *Shattered societies, shattered lives: Refugee women and their mental health.* New York: Haworth Press.

De La Cancela, V. (1985). Toward a sociocultural psychotherapy for low-income ethnic minorities. *Psychotherapy: Theory, Research and Practice, 22,* 427–435.

Denzin, N. K. (1989). *Interpretive interactionism* Newbury Park, CA: Sage.

Easterlin, R. A., Ward, D., Bernard, W. S., & Ueda, R. (1982). *Immigration.* Cambridge, MA: Harvard University Press.

Edwards, J. (1985). *Language, society, and identity.* New York: Basil Blackwell.

Erikson, E. H. (1964). *Insight and responsibility.* New York: Norton.

Erikson, E. H. (1975). *Life history and the historical moment.* New York: Norton.

Espín, O. M. (1984). Cultural and historical influences on sexuality in Hispanic/Latin women. In C. Vance (Ed.), *Pleasure and danger: Exploring female sexuality* (pp. 149–164). London: Routledge and Kegan Paul. [Also in Espín, O. M. (1997). *Latina realities: Essays on healing, migration, and sexuality* (pp. 83–96). Boulder, CO: Westview Press.]

Espín, O. M. (1987a). Issues of identity in the psychology of Latina lesbians. In Boston Lesbian Psychologies Collective (Eds.), *Lesbian psychologies: Explorations and challenges* (pp. 35–55). Urbana: University of Illinois Press. [Also in Espín, O. M. (1997). *Latina realities: Essays on healing, migration, and sexuality* (pp. 97–109). Boulder, CO: Westview Press.]

Espín, O. M. (1987b). Psychological impact of migration on Latinas: Implications for psychotherapeutic practice. *Psychology of Women Quarterly, 11*(4), 489–503. [Also in Espín, O. M. (1997). *Latina realities: Essays on healing, migration, and sexuality* (pp. 115–128). Boulder, CO: Westview Press.]

Espín, O. M. (1992). Roots uprooted: The psychological impact of historical/political dislocation. In E. Cole, O. M. Espín, & E. Rothblum (Eds.), *Refugee women and their mental health: Shattered societies, shattered lives* (pp. 9–20). New York: Haworth Press.

Espín, O. M. (1994a). Feminist approaches [to therapy with women of color]. In L. Comas-Díaz & B. Greene (Eds.), *Women of color and mental health* (pp. 265–286). New York: Guilford. [Also in Espín, O. M. (1997). *Latina realities: Essays on healing, migration, and sexuality* (pp. 51–70). Boulder, CO: Westview Press.]

Espín, O. M. (1994b). Traumatic historical events and adolescent psychosocial development: Letters from V. In C. Franz & A. J. Stewart (Eds.), *Women creating lives: Identities, resilience, and resistance* (pp. 187–198). Boulder, CO: Westview Press. [Also in Espín, O. M. (1997) *Latina reali-*

ties: Essays on healing, migration, and sexuality (pp. 144–156). Boulder, CO: Westview Press.]

Espín, O. M. (1995). "Race," racism, and sexuality in the life narratives of immigrant women. *Feminism and Psychology, 5*(2), 223–238. [Also in Espín, O. M. (1997). *Latina realities: Essays on healing, migration, and sexuality* (pp. 171–185). Boulder, CO: Westview Press.]

Espín, O. M. (1996a). Crossing borders and boundaries: Gender and sexuality in the life narratives of immigrant women. In E. Olstein & G. Horenczyk (Eds.), *Language, identity, and immigration*. Jerusalem, Israel: Magnes Press.

Espín, O.M. (1996b). *Latina healers: Lives of power and tradition*. Encino, CA: Floricanto Press.

Espín, O. M. (1996c). Leaving the nation and joining the tribe: Lesbian immigrants crossing geographical and identity borders. *Women and Therapy, 19*(4), 99–107. [Also in Espín, O. M. (1997). *Latina realities: Essays on healing, migration, and sexuality* (pp. 186–193). Boulder, CO: Westview Press.]

Espín, O. M. (1997). *Latina realities: Essays on healing, migration, and sexuality*. Boulder, CO: Westview Press.

Espín, O. M. (1999). Immigration. In B. Zimmerman (Ed.). *The encyclopedia of lesbian histories and cultures*. New York: Garland.

Espín, O. M., Cavanaugh, A., Paydarfar, N. & Wood, R. (1990, March). *Mothers, daughters, and migration: A new look at the psychology of separation*. Paper presented at the Annual Meeting of the Association for Women in Psychology, Tempe, AZ.

Espín, O. M., Stewart, A. J. & Gómez, C. (1990). Letters from V. : Adolescent personality development in socio-historical context. *Journal of Personality, 58*, 347–364. [Also in Espín, O. M. (1997). *Latina realities: Essays on healing, migration, and sexuality* (pp. 129–143). Boulder, CO: Westview Press.]

Essed, P. (1991). *Understanding everyday racism*. Newbury Park, CA: Sage.

Essed, P. (1994). Contradictory positions, ambivalent perceptions: A case study of a Black woman entrepreneur. *Feminism & Psychology, 4*(1), 99–118.

Fernea, E. W., & Fernea, R. A. (1995). Symbolizing roles: Behind the veil. In M. E. Roach-Higgins, J. B. Eicher, & K. K. P. Johnson (Eds.), *Dress and Identity* (pp. 285–292). New York: Fairchild Publications.

Figley, C. R. (Ed.). (1985). *Trauma and its wake: The study and treatment of post-traumatic stress disorder*. New York: Brunner/Mazel.

Fishman, J. A., Cooper, R. L., & Ma, R. (1975). *Bilingualism in the barrio*. Bloomington, IN: University of Indiana Press.

Foss, R. J. (1994). The demise of the homosexual exclusion: New possibilities for gay and lesbian immigration. *Harvard Civil Rights–Civil Liberties Law Review, 29*, 439–475.

Foucault, M. (1981). *The history of sexuality*. Harmondsworth: Penguin.

Franz, C. E., & Stewart, A. J. (Eds.). (1994). *Women creating lives: Identities, resilience, and resistance*. Boulder, CO: Westview Press.

Gabaccia, D. (Ed.). (1992). *Seeking common ground: Multidisciplinary studies of immigrant women in the United States*. Westport, CT: Praeger.

Gabaccia, D. (1994). *From the other side: Women, gender & immigrant life in the U. S., 1820–1990*. Bloomington, IN: Indiana University Press.

Gagnon, J. H. (1992). The self, its voices, and their discord. In C. Ellis & M. Flagerty (Eds.). *Investigating subjectivity: Research on lived experience* (pp. 221–243). Newbury Park, CA: Sage.

Garza-Guerrero, C. (1974). Culture shock: Its mourning and the vicissitudes of identity. *Journal of the American Psychoanalytic Association, 22*, 408–429.

Gay, J. (1993). "Mummies and babies" and friends and lovers in Lesotho. In D. N. Suggs & A. W. Miracle (Eds.), *Culture and human sexuality* (pp. 341–355). Belmont, CA: Wadsworth.

Ginorio, A. (1979). A comparison of Puerto Ricans in New York with native Puerto Ricans and Caucasian- and Black-Americans on two measures of acculturation: Gender role and racial identification. (Doctoral dissertation, Fordham University.) *Dissertation Abstracts International, 40*, 983B–984B.

González-Reigosa, F. (1976). The anxiety-arousing effect of taboo words in bilinguals. In C. D. Spielberger & R. Diaz-Gurrero (Eds.), *Cross-cultural anxiety* (pp. 309–326). Washington, DC: Hemisphere.

Goodenow, C., & Espín, O. M. (1993). Identity choices in immigrant female adolescents. *Adolescence, 28*, 173–184.

Grinberg, L., & Grinberg, R. (1984). *Psicoanálisis de la migración y del exilio*. Madrid: Alianza Editorial. [English translation by N. Festinger. *Psychoanalytic perspectives on migration and exile*. New Haven, Yale University Press, 1989.]

Hartmann, H. (1964). *Essays on ego psychology*. New York: International Universities Press.

Havens, L. (1986). *Making contact: Uses of language in psychotherapy*. Cambridge, MA: Harvard University Press.

Hirsch, M. (1994). Pictures of a displaced childhood. In A. Bammer (Ed.), *Displacements: Cultural identities in question* (pp. 71–89). Bloomington: Indiana University Press.

Ho, C. K. (1990). An analysis of domestic violence in Asian American communities: A multicultural approach to counseling. In L. S. Brown & M. P. P. Root (Eds.), *Diversity and complexity in feminist therapy* (pp. 129–150). New York: Harrington Park Press.

Hoffman, E. (1989). *Lost in translation*. New York: Dutton.

Hondagneu-Sotelo, P. (1992). Overcoming patriarchal constraints: The reconstruction of gender relations among Mexican immigrant women and men. *Gender & Society, 6*(3), 393–415.

Hondagneu-Sotelo, P. (1994). *Gendered transitions: Mexican experiences of immigration*. Berkeley: University of California Press.

Hymes, D. H. (1961). *Linguistic aspects of cross-cultural personality theory: Studying personality cross-culturally*. New York: Harper & Row.

Jaggar, A., & Bordo, S. (Eds.). (1989). *Gender/Body/Knowledge*. New Brunswick, NJ: Rutgers University Press.

Javier, R. (1989). Linguistic consideration in the treatment of bilinguals. *Psychoanalytic Psychology, 6* (1), 87–96.

Javier, R. S., Barroso, F., & Muñoz, M. (1993). Autobiographical memory in bilinguals. *Journal of Psycholinguistic Research, 22*(3), 319–338.

Josselson, R. (1996). On writing other people's lives: Self-analytic reflections of a narrative researcher. *The narrative study of lives* (Vol. 4, pp. 60–71). Thousand Oaks, CA: Sage.

Josselson, R., & Lieblich, A. (Eds.). (1993). *The narrative study of lives*. Newbury Park, CA: Sage.

Kallifatides, H. (1992, May). *Language and identity*. Paper presented at the annual meeting of the Society for the Advancement of Scandinavian Studies, Minneapolis, MN.

Kaschak, E. (1992). *Engendered lives*. N. Y. : Basic Books.

Kibria, N. (1990). Power, patriarchy, and gender conflict in the Vietnamese immigrant community. *Gender & Society, 4*(1), 9–24.

Krapf, E. E. (1955). The choice of language in polyglot psychoanalysis. *Psychoanalytic Quarterly, 24*, 343–357.

Krueger, R. A. (1994). *Focus groups: A practical guide for applied research* (2nd ed.). Thousand Oaks, CA: Sage.

Kvale, S. (1983). The qualitative research interview: A phenomenological and hermeneutical mode of understanding. *Journal of Phenomenological Psychology, 14*(2), 171–196.

Kvale, S. (1996). *InterViews*. Thousand Oaks, CA: Sage.

Laqueur, T. (1990). *Making sex: Body and gender from the Greeks to Freud.* Cambridge, MA: Harvard University Press.

Levy-Warren, M. H. (1987). Moving to a new culture: Cultural identity, loss, and mourning. In J. Bloom-Feshbach & S. Bloom-Feshbach (Eds.), *The psychology of separation and loss: Perspectives on development, life transitions, and clinical practice* (pp. 300–315). San Francisco: Jossey-Bass.

Lieblich, A. (1993). Looking at change. Natasha, 21: New immigrant from Russia to Israel. In R. Josselson & A. Lieblich (Eds.), (1993). *The narrative study of lives* (pp. 92–129). Newbury Park, CA: Sage.

Lindemann, E. (1944). Symptomatology and management of acute grief. *American Journal of Psychiatry, 101*,141–148.

Lorde, A. (1984). *Sister outsider*. Freedom, CA: Crossing Press.

Mahler, S. J. (1995). *American dreaming: Immigrant lives on the margins.* Princeton, NJ: Princeton University Press.

Marcos, L. (1976a). Bilinguals in psychotherapy: Language as an emotional barrier. *American Journal of Psychotherapy, 30*, 522–560.

Marcos, L. (1976b). Bilingualism and sense of self. *American Journal of Psychoanalysis, 37*, 285–290.

Marcos, L. R., & Alpert, M. (1976) Strategies and risks in psychotherapy with bilingual patients: The phenomenon of language independence. *American Journal of Psychiatry, 133*, 1275–1278.

Marcos, L. R., & Urcuyo, L. (1979). Dynamic psychotherapy with the bilingual patient. *American Journal of Psychotherapy, 33*, 331–338.

Marín, B. V., Marín, G., Juárez, R., & Sorensen, J. L. (1992). Intervention from family members as a strategy for preventing HIV among intravenous drug users. *Journal of Community Psychology, 20*, 90–97.

Marín, B. V., Tschann, J. M., Gómez, C. A., & Kegeles, S. M. (1993). Acculturation and gender differences in sexual attitudes and behaviors: Hispanic vs. non-Hispanic white unmarried adults. *American Journal of Public Health, 83*, 1759–1761.

Marris, P. (1986). *Loss and change*. London: Routledge and Kegan Paul.

McAdams, D. (1990). Unity and purpose in human lives: The emergence of identity as a life story. In A. Rabin, R. A. Zucker, R. A. Emmons & S. Frank (Eds.), *Studying persons and lives* (pp. 148–200). New York: Springer.

Mishler, E. G. (1986). *Research interviewing: Context and narrative*. Cambridge, MA: Harvard University Press.

Mishler, E. G. (1995). Models of narrative analysis: A typology. *Journal of Narrative and Life History, 5*(2), 87–123.

Molesky, J. (1986). The exiled: Pathology of Central American refugees. *Migration World, 14*(4), 19–23.

Morgan, D. L. (1988). *Focus groups as qualitative research*. Newbury Park, CA: Sage.

Morgan, D. L. (Ed.). (1993). *Successful focus groups*. Newbury Park, CA: Sage.

Murray, H. (1938). *Explorations in personality*. New York: Oxford University Press.

Narayan, U. (1995). "Male-order" brides: Immigrant women, domestic violence, and immigrations law. *Hypathia*, 10(1), 104–119.

Narayan, U. (1997). *Dislocating cultures: Identities, traditions, and Third World feminism*. New York: Routledge.

Nathanson, C. A. (1991). *Dangerous passage: The social control of sexuality in women's adolescence*. Philadelphia: Temple University Press.

Necef, M. U. (1994). The language of intimacy. In L. E. Andersen (Ed.) *Middle East studies in Denmark* (pp. 141–158). Odense, Denmark: Odense University Press.

Obejas, A. (1994). *We came all the way from Cuba so you could dress like this?* Pittsburgh, PA: Cleis Press.

Ochberg, R. L. (1992). Social insight and psychological liberation. In G. C. Rosenwald & R. L. Ochberg (Eds.), *Storied lives: The cultural politics of self-understanding* (pp. 214–230). New Haven, CT: Yale University Press.

Ochberg, R. L. (1996). Interpreting life stories. In R. Josselson (Ed.), *The narrative study of lives* (Vol. 4, pp. 97–113). Thousand Oaks, CA: Sage.

Odeh, L. A. (1993). Post-colonial feminism and the veil: Thinking the difference. *Feminist Review, 43*, 26–37.

Ogundipe-Leslie, 'M. (1993). African women, culture and another development. In S. M. James & A. P. A. Busia (Eds.), *Theorizing Black feminisms* (pp. 102–117). London: Routledge.

Paris, J. (1978). The symbolic return: Psychodynamic aspects of immigration and exile. *Journal of the American Academy of Psychoanalysis, 6*, 51–57.

Park, J. S. (1995). Pink asylum: Political asylum eligibility or gay men and lesbians under U.S. immigration policy. *UCLA Law Review, 42*, 1115–1156.

Parker, A., Russo, M., Sommer, D., & Yaeger, P. (Eds.) (1992). *Nationalisms and sexualities.* New York: Routledge.

Parker, R. G., & Gagnon, J. H. (1995). *Conceiving sexuality: Approaches to sex research in a post-modern world.* New York: Routledge.

Parkes, L. M. (1975). *Bereavement: Studies in grief in adult life.* New York: International Universities Press.

Pedraza, S. (1991). Women and migration: The social consequences of gender. *Annual Review of Sociology, 17*, 303–325.

Pedraza, S., & Rumbaut, R. G. (1996). *Origins and destinies: Immigration, race, and ethnicity in America.* Belmont, CA: Wadsworth.

Phizacklea, A. (Ed.). (1983). *One way ticket: Migration and female labour.* London: Routledge & Kegan Paul.

Plummer, K. (1995). *Telling sexual stories: Power, change, and social worlds.* London: Routledge.

Polkinghorne, D. E. (1988). *Narrative knowing and the human sciences.* Albany, NY: State University of New York Press.

Portes, A., & Rumbaut, R. G. (1996). *Immigrant America: A portrait* (2nd ed.). Berkeley, CA: University of California Press.

Prieto, Y. (1992). Cuban women in New Jersey: Gender relations and change. In D. Gabaccia (Ed.), *Seeking common ground: Multidisciplinary studies of immigrant women in the United States* (pp. 185–201). Westport, CT: Greenwood Press.

Renzetti, C. M., & Lee, R. M. (Eds.). (1993). *Researching Sensitive Topics.* Newbury Park, CA: Sage.

Richmond, A. H. (1994). *Global apartheid: Refugees, racism, and the new world order.* Oxford, UK: Oxford University Press.

Riessman, C. K. (1993). *Narrative analysis.* Newbury Park, CA: Sage.

Roach-Higgins, M. E., Eicher, J. B., & Johnson, K. K. P. (Eds.), *Dress and Identity.* New York: Fairchild Publications.

Roberts, G. W., & Sinclair, S. A. (1978). *Women in Jamaica: Patterns of reproduction and family*. Milwood, NY: KTO Press.

Rodríguez-Nogués, L. (1983). Psychological effects of premature separation from parents in Cuban refugee girls: A retrospective study. (Doctoral dissertation, Boston University.) *Dissertation Abstracts International, 44,* 1619B.

Rogler, L. H. (1994). International migrations: A framework for directing research. *American Psychologist, 49* (8), 701–708.

Rosensky, R., & Gómez, M. (1983). Language switch in psychotherapy with bilinguals: Two problems, two models and case examples. *Psychotherapy: Theory, Research and Practice, 20,* 152–160.

Rosenwald, G. C. (1988). A theory of multiple-case research. *Journal of Personality, 56*(1), 239–264.

Rosenwald, G. C. (1992). Conclusion: Reflections on narrative self-understanding. In G. C. Rosenwald & R. L. Ochberg (Eds.), *Storied lives: The cultural politics of self-understanding* (pp. 265–289). New Haven, CT: Yale University Press.

Rosenwald, G. C. (1996). Making whole: Method and ethics in mainstream and narrative psychology. In R. Josselson (Ed.), *The narrative study of lives* (Vol. 4, pp. 245–274). Thousand Oaks, CA: Sage.

Rosenwald, G. C., & Ochberg, R. L. (1992). *Storied lives: The cultural politics of self-understanding*. New Haven, CT: Yale University Press.

Rubin, H. J., & Rubin, I. S. (1995). *Qualitative Interviewing: The art of hearing data*. Thousand Oaks, CA: Sage.

Ruiz, V. L. (1992). The flapper and the chaperone: Historical memory among Mexican-American women. In D. Gabaccia (Ed.), *Seeking common ground: Multidisciplinary studies of immigrant women in the United States* (pp. 141–157). Westport, CT: Praeger.

Sahgal, G., & Yuval-Davis, N. (1992). Introduction: Fundamentalism, multiculturalism and women in Britain. In *Refusing Holy Orders: Women and fundamentalism in Britain* (pp. 1–25). London: Virago Press.

Salgado de Snyder, V. N. (1986). *Mexican immigrant women: The relationship of ethnic loyalty, self-esteem, social support, and satisfaction to acculturative stress and depressive symptomatology*. Doctoral dissertation, University of California, Los Angeles.

Salgado de Snyder, V. N., Cervantes, R. C., & Padilla, A. M. (1990). Gender and ethnic differences in psychosocial stress and generalized distress among Hispanics. *Sex Roles, 22*(7/8), 441–453.

Sarbin, T. (Ed.). (1986). *Narrative psychology: The storied nature of human conduct*. New York: Praeger.

Schreier, B. A. (1994). *Becoming American women: Clothing and the Jewish immigrant experience, 1880–1920*. Chicago: Chicago Historical Society.

Silverman, D. (1993). *Interpreting qualitative data: Methods for analyzing talk, text, and interaction*. London: Sage.

Smith, J. A., Harré, R., & Langenhove, I. V. (Eds.). (1995). *Rethinking methods in psychology*. London: Sage.

Stewart, A. J. (1994). The women's movement and women's lives: Linking individual development and social events. In R. Josselson (Ed.), *The narrative study of lives* (Vol. 2, pp. 230–250). Thousand Oaks, CA: Sage.

Stewart, D. W., & Shamdasani, P. N. (1990). *Focus groups: Theory and practice*. Newbury Park, CA: Sage.

Stonequist, E. V. (1937). The problem of the marginal man. *American Journal of Sociology, 41*(1), 1–12.

Strauss, A. L. (1987). *Qualitative analysis for social scientists*. Cambridge, England: Cambridge University Press.

Szapocznik, J., & Kurtines, W. (1980). Acculturation, biculturalism and adjustment among Cuban Americans. In A. Padilla (Ed.), *Acculturation: Theory models and some new findings* (pp. 139–159). Boulder, CO: Westview Press.

Taft, R. (1977). Coping with unfamiliar cultures. In N. Warren (Ed.), *Studies in cross-cultural psychology* (pp. 121–153). New York: Academic Press.

Telles, P. (1980, March). *The psychosocial effects of immigration upon aging Cuban women*. Paper presented at the National Hispanic Feminist Conference, San Jose, CA.

Thomas, W. I., & Znaniecki, F. (1918–1920/1927). *The Polish peasant in Europe and America*. Boston: Richard C. Badger and New York: A. Knopf.

Todd, E. (1994). *Le destin des immigrés: Assimilation et ségrégation dans les démocraties occidentales*. [The destiny of immigrants: Assimilation and segregation in Western democracies.] Paris: Editions du Seuil.

Tohidi, N. (1991). Gender and Islamic fundamentalism: Feminist politics in Iran. In C. T. Mohanty, A. Russo, & L. Torres (Eds.). *Third World women and the politics of feminism* (pp. 251–270). Bloomington, IN: Indiana University Press.

Torres, L. (1991). The construction of the self in U. S. Latina autobiographies. In C. T. Mohanty, A. Russo, & L. Torres (Eds.), *Third World women and the politics of feminism* (pp. 271–287). Bloomington, IN: Indiana University Press.

Torres-Matrullo, C. (1980). Acculturation, sex-role values and mental health among mainland Puerto Ricans. In A. Padilla (Ed.), *Acculturation: Theory, models and some new findings* (pp. 111–137). Boulder, CO: Westview Press.

Tremble, B., Schneider, M., & Appathurai, C. (1989). Growing up gay or lesbian in multicultural context. In G. Herdt (Ed.), *Gay and lesbian youth* (pp. 253–267). New York: Harrington Park Press.

Trumbach, R. (1977). London's sodomites. *Journal of Social History, 11*, 1–33.

United Nations Expert Group Meeting on International Migration Policies and the Status of Female Migrants (U.N.-IMPSF). (1995). *International migration policies and the status of female migrants.* New York: United Nations.

United Nations High Commission for Refugees (UNHCR). (1997). *The state of the world's refugees: A humanitarian agenda.* New York: United Nations.

United Nations International Research and Training Institute for the Advancement of Women (U.N.-INSTRAW). (1994). *The migration of women: Methodological issues in the measurement and analysis of internal and international migration.* New York: United Nations.

U. S. Committee for Refugees. (1990). *World refugee survey: 1989 in review.* Washington, DC: American Council for Nationalities.

Valverde, M. (1985). *Sex, power, and pleasure.* Toronto: Women's Press.

Weiss, R. S. (1994). *Learning from strangers.* Toronto: Free Press.

White, R. (1966). *Lives in progress* (2nd ed.). New York: Holt, Rinehart & Winston.

Wierzbicka, A. (1994). Emotion, language, and cultural scripts. In S. Kitayama & H. R. Markus (Eds.). *Emotion and culture* (pp. 133–196). Washington, DC: American Psychological Association.

Woollett, A., Marshall, H., Nicholson, P., & Dosanjh, N. (1994). Asian women's ethnic identity: The impact of gender and context in the accounts of women bringing up children in East London. *Feminism & Psychology, 4* (1), 119–132.

Yuval-Davis, N. (1992). Fundamentalism, multiculturalism and women in Britain. In J. Donald & A. Rattansi (Eds.), *Race, culture, and difference* (pp. 278–291). London: Sage.

Index

abortion, 90–91
abuse, *see* domestic violence; rape; sexual abuse
Accad, E., 123
accents (pronunciation), 72–73, 74–75, 133, 134, 140, 165
see also language
acculturation process
  age impacting, 22–23, 118–21, 146, 164, 165
  assimilation vs., 21
  clothing and, *see* clothing
  context of exit from home culture and, 16, 21, 28–29
  gender roles and, 23–27, 74, 75, 125, 163, 165
  language and, 89, 90
  for lesbians, 154, 156–57, 158–59
  mourning losses and, 30
  psychological stages of, 20–23
  racism affecting, 9–10, 22, 27–28, 71–75, 164
  social status of women and, 4
  traumatic experiences affecting, 28–29
  women's sexual behavior and, 6–7, 74, 76, 78, 82, 125, 128–32, 164
see also identity

adaptation, *see* acculturation process
adolescents
  acculturation process and, 22, 24, 118–21, 146
  adaptation to sex roles from two cultures, 9–10, 164
  coming out as lesbians, 157, 158
  language for sexuality, 142, 144
  rebelliousness of, 25, 36 n2, 75
  separation from parents through immigration, 12–13, 26–27, 32, 49, 55, 112–18, 148–49
  study of impacts of migration on, 11–12, 49, 50, 55, 118–21
African Americans, 72–75
  see also racism
age
  impacting acculturation process, 22–23, 118–21, 146, 164, 165
  of interviewees, 48, 49, 50–51
  see also adolescents; children
AIDS, 129, 147, 166
alienation, 19, 27
anger
  of children toward parents, 27, 32, 81–82
anger (*cont.*)
  in grieving process, 31
  see also domestic violence

anxiety
  bilingual coping mechanisms for, 136
  in grieving process, 31
  taboo words and, 138
apathy, in grieving process, 31
Appathurai, C., 157
appearance
  clothing, 71, 96, 114, 125–28
  eating disorders, 93–94
  importance of, 65, 120
  obesity, 85, 86, 89
appetite loss, in grieving process, 31
assimilation, acculturation vs., 21
authority
  perceived disrespect for, in U. S., 73, 112
  language and subversion of, 135
  of men, 8, 24, 76–77
  rebellion against parents, 25, 36 n2, 75
  see also power
autonomy, impacts of migration on, 3
"average expectable" environment, 30, 31

Bammer, Angelika, 134, 150
Bandura, Albert, 35
Barroso, F., 139
Bar-Yam, A., 11
Basch, C. E., 43–44
Becoming American Women: Clothing and the Jewish Immigrant Experience, 1880–1920 (Schreier), 126
bereavement, migration experience compared to, 31–32
betrayal, to homeland loyalties, 33, 71, 135, 158
Bhavnani, K.-K., 10, 159
bilingualism, *see* language
Boszormenyi-Nagy, I., 33
Caplan, P., 132
Cervantes, R. C., 18

children
  acculturation process and, 22, 24, 165
  anger toward parents, 27, 32, 81–82
  born outside of marriage, 59
  language proficiency in, 22, 24, 134–35
  percentage of, as refugees, 3
  see also adolescents
circumcision, female, 36 n1, 59
class, socioeconomic
  of immigrants to U. S., 46–47
  loss of, through immigration, 92
  maintenance of, 22
clothing, 96, 114
  and sexuality, 71, 125–28
coming out process
  acculturation process and, 158–59
  for adolescents, 157, 158
  to children, 88, 149–50
  in home culture, 75
  immigration facilitating, 77–78, 81–82, 87–89, 104, 116, 165
  parents' reactions to, 65–67, 82–83, 87, 88–89, 116, 149, 157, 158
  racism and, 156, 158–59
  religion and, 64, 76
communication, *see* language
conflicts
  about sexual orientation, 158
  adolescence magnifying, 164
  clothing purchases within families, 128
  gender roles within families, 22–24, 45, 59, 60, 71, 130–31, 150
  refusal to adapt to host culture, 22, 120–21
  resolution of, through new identity, 135
  unresolved through separation, 27, 32
control
  of men in sexual act, 106, 124

of women to maintain tradition, 6–8, 13, 124, 129, 149

country of birth, *see* home culture

country of reception, *see* host culture

cultural sensitivity, oppression through guise of, 8–9

cultural values, *see* tradition; values

daughters
  abandonment by mother, 95, 96–97
  coming out as lesbian to parents, 65–67, 82–83, 87, 88–89, 116, 149, 157, 158
  fear of sexuality, 60, 148
  migration away from families, *see* single women
  mothers' impact on identity development of, 145–46, 163–64
  patriarchal context of relationship with mothers, 76–77, 151, 164
  sexual behavior measuring family morality, 6, 45
  study of impacts of migration on, 11–12, 49, 50, 55, 118–21
  study on separation from mothers, 12–13, 49, 55, 112–18, 148–49
  see also adolescents; families; mothers; narratives

defense mechanisms, traditional behaviors as, 6, 22

denial
  of domestic violence, 130
  due to separation, 27, 32
  grieving process and, 31

depression, 28, 32, 107, 150

disillusionment, during acculturation process, 20

divorce, from influence of migration, 97

domestic violence, 62–63, 64, 77, 100
  cultural tolerance of, 9, 59, 129–30, 132 n2
  see also rape

Dosanjh, N., 126–27

drug abuse, 22, 112

eating disorders, 93–94
  see also obesity

economic gain, as motivation for migration, 16

education
  affecting acculturation process, 27–28
  increased access to, 4, 19, 23

elders, protection of cultural values by, 23–24

emotions
  language and, 94, 95–96, 136–37, 138–39, 142–43, 165–66
  see also language and sexuality

employment
  downward mobility in, 28
  increased access to, 4, 19, 23, 24

Erickson, E. H., 24–25

Essed, Philomena, 8

exogamy, as indicator of successful migration, 4

families
  conflicts over clothing purchases, 128
  conflicts over gender roles, 22–24, 45, 59, 60, 71, 130–31, 150
  double standards in, 59, 60, 68, 74, 75, 87, 129
  immigration policies and, 73
  intergenerational transmission of trauma, 15–16, 86
  language issues in, 22, 24, 134–35
  lesbians coming out to, 65–67, 82–83, 87, 88–89, 116, 149–50, 157, 158
  male-female power relations in, 6, 18, 19, 23, 69, 74, 76–77, 92
families (*cont.*)
  migration away from, *see* single women
  morality of, measured through

women's sexual behavior, 6, 45
need for cultural displacement
  model for, 150
reunification of, as motivation for
  migration, 16, 17
sexual abuse in, 87, 129
unresolved conflicts through separation, 27, 32
violence within, 9, 62–63, 64, 77,
  100, 129–30, 132 n2
see also adolescents; children;
  daughters; fathers; mothers;
  parents
fathers
  acceptance of lesbian daughters,
    66–67, 82
  aggression/violence of, 62–63, 64,
    77, 129–30, 132 n2
  as role models, 77, 164
  separation from daughters, 149
  see also families; parents
feminists
  lesbian, 61, 130
  in Turkey, 100
  within immigrant communities, 94,
    130, 150–51
feminist scholarship, 40–41
Fernea, E. W., 126
Fernea, R. A., 126
focus groups, 43–44, 45–46, 49,
  56–57
Foss, R. J., 154–55
Freud, Sigmund, 37, 38
friendship networks
  difficulty establishing, 59, 113, 115,
    120–21
  importance of, 60, 61, 63, 150
  loss of, 6, 18, 19, 24, 29, 159
Gabaccia, Donna, 10, 47, 73, 150
gay men, 62, 132 n.1, 154
gendered racism, 8
  see also racism
gender roles
  acceptance of traditional, 7, 23, 92

acculturation process and, 23–27,
  74, 75, 125, 163, 165
double standards in, 59, 60, 68, 74,
  75, 87, 129
family conflicts over, 22–24, 45, 59,
  60, 71, 130–31, 150
modification of, through migration,
  4–5, 20, 109
preserving tradition through, 6–7,
  149
racism impacting, *see* racism
resulting in isolation of women,
  22
study of development and transformation of, 11, 45, 48, 49, 55, 56
transmission of, through mothers,
  2, 125, 146–48
genital mutilation, 36 n1, 59
geographical place, importance of,
  33–35
González-Reigosa, F., 138
Goodenow, C., 9, 25
grief, 16
  psychological impacts of, 30–33
  see also loss; mourning
Grinberg, L., 134, 135
Grinberg, R., 134, 135
guilt feelings
  from betrayal of loyalties, 33, 135,
    158
  of children toward parents, 27
  in grieving process, 31
  from lesbian orientation, 66, 76
  from sexual abuse/rape, 28

Haraway, D., 10
health, physical, 129, 146–47, 150, 166
heterosexuals
  attitudes of lesbian feminists vs.,
    61
  language and, 58–59, 142, 158
  percentage of interviewees, 53
Hirsch, Marianne, 150–51
HIV, 129, 147, 166

Ho, Christine, 9
Hoffman, Eva, 133, 141
home culture
    acculturation eradicating values
        of, 21
    defined, 6
    gender differences in desire to
        return to, 24
    idealization of, 23, 30–31,
        120–21
    internalization of cultural norms
        of, 5
    motivations for migration from,
        16–18, 28–29
    periodic visits to, 21, 26–27, 28, 34,
        79, 86
    persecution for sexual orientation
        in, 75, 154, 155, 156
    pressure to conform to tradition
        within, 6–8, 123–25
    psychological stress from loss of,
        29–33
    social status impacting migration
        from, 4
homosexuality, *see* gay men; lesbians
Hondagneu-Sotelo, P., 10, 163
host culture
    defined, 4
    immigrant communities in, *see*
        immigrant communities
    prejudice against traditional cloth-
        ing, 114
    racism in, *see* racism
    rejection of, as coping mechanism,
        22, 120–21
    sadness equated with ingratitude
        by, 30
    social status impacting successful
        migration, 4
    see also United States

identity
    adolescents' separation from par-
        ents and, 26–27, 112–18, 148–49

betrayal of homeland loyalties and,
        33, 71, 135, 158
    clothing and, *see* clothing
    cultural norms forming, 5
    gender differences in adapting, 7,
        9–10, 19, 162–66
    language and transformation of,
        133–38, 139–41, 142–44
    loss of cultural, 22, 91, 93, 96, 99,
        112, 119, 133–36
    loss of family/friends and, 6, 24
    maintenance of social status and,
        22, 28
    mother-daughter relationship and,
        145–46, 163–64
    mourning former, 30
    questioning what could have been,
        33–35, 111, 157–58
    see also acculturation; sexuality
illegitimacy, 59
Immigrant America: A Portrait (Portes
    & Rumbaut), 17
immigrant communities
    easing transition, 119
    expectations of sexuality and gen-
        der roles in, 6, 8, 76, 78, 101,
        124–25, 128–32
    feminists within, 94, 130, 150–51
    guardians of morality in, 6–7, 124–25
    reactions to homosexuality in, 76,
        153, 154, 157
    single women within, 26
    women's status and successful
        migration, 4
immigrants
    refugees vs., 16–18
    term usage, 17, 18
Immigration Act of 1917, 154
Immigration Act of 1990, 155
Immigration and Nationality Act
    (INA) (1952), 154–55
Immigration and Naturalization Ser-
    vice (INS), 155, 156
immigration policies

families and, 73
sexual orientation and, 154–56
incest, 87, 129
insomnia, in grieving process, 31
integration, social, as indicator of successful migration, 4
internalization
of cultural norms, 5
of oppression, 8
interview process
comfort/discomfort when addressing sexuality, 45, 67, 138–39, 141–42
methodology, 42–46
in narrative research, 40–41, 47, 53–54, 56–57, 162
role of language, 11, 44–46, 47, 56, 63, 67
sample, 11, 12, 41, 46–54, 55–56
text for, 167–70
see also narratives
invisible loyalties, 33
isolation, 22, 150
see also friendship networks, loss of

Javier, Rafael, 136, 139

Kallifatides, Theodor, 140
Kvale, S., 44–45

language
and acculturation, 89, 90
adolescent rebellion against first, 25
for affection, 78, 83, 88, 95–96, 104
capacity for intimacy and use of, 165–66
children's proficiency in, 22, 24, 134–35
gradual loss of first, 97–98
identity loss and recreation through, 133–38, 139–41, 142–44
memory and, 139
prior knowledge of host culture, 22

psychotherapy and, 136–37, 139, 141
role of, in interview process, 11, 44–46, 47, 56, 63, 67
language and sexuality, 138–39, 141–44
difficulties communicating with peers about, 59–60, 62, 101
preference for first language, 76, 109
preference for second language, 67, 70, 78, 80, 83, 87, 92–93, 94, 101, 106
use of both first and second languages, 85–86, 88, 98, 102, 104
see also mothers, sexual information supplied by; mothers, sexual information withheld by
Lee, R. M., 41
Lesbian and Gay Immigration Rights Task Force, 155–56
lesbians
acculturation process for, 154, 156–57, 158–59
affection vs. sexual relations, 64–65, 83
Aurelia (Australia/Thailand), 81–83, 89, 143
Cecilia (Puerto Rico), 87–89, 149–50
Cindy (Taiwan), 79–81, 89, 149, 158
clothing issues, 127
coming out process, *see* coming out process
Eva (Austria), 84–86, 89, 149
feminists, 61, 130
guilt feelings of, 66, 76
immigration policies and, 154–56
impacts of cultural traditions on, 124
lacking awareness of existence of, 60–61, 65, 111
Liv (Denmark), 110, 111–12
Lorena (Puerto Rica), 76–79, 89, 139, 142, 156, 158

Maritza (Cuba), 75–76, 88, 142, 149, 156, 158
Maya (Netherlands), 86–87, 89, 144, 149, 156
Olga (Cuba), 75, 76, 88, 156, 158
percentage of interviewees, 53
regretting sexual orientation, 66
rejection of, in immigrant communities, 153, 154, 157
Soledad (Brazil), 103–4
transformation of sexuality through migration, 5, 76, 77–78, 82, 85–86, 88–89, 101, 131, 156, 157–58
Ursula (Germany), 56, 64–67, 142, 144, 149
use of language by bilingual, 67, 76, 78, 80, 83, 85–86, 87, 88, 104, 139, 142, 158
Violeta (Cuba), 12, 112, 116, 148, 149, 151
Levy-Warren, M. H., 21
loneliness, 19, 25–26, 115, 116, 121
Lorde, Audre, 131
loss
    of cultural identity, 22, 91, 93, 96, 99, 112, 119, 133–36
    of friendship networks, 6, 18, 19, 24, 29, 159
    psychological impacts of, 27, 29–33, 107
    questioning what could have been, 33–35, 111, 157–58
    of status, 8, 24, 74, 92
    see also grief
Lost in Translation (Hoffman), 133
loyalties, betrayal of homeland, 33, 71, 135, 158
McAdams, D., 38
male superiority
    attempts to uphold tradition through, 6–7, 8, 124–25, 128–32
    in U. S., 150
Marcos, Luis, 137
"marginal man," 22

marriage
    arranged, 71, 98, 113–14
    interracial, 4, 91, 94, 106, 165–66
    rejection of, 102
    same-sex, 156
    see also romantic relationships
Marris, Peter, 30, 31, 32, 33
Marshall, H., 126–27
memories, linguistic organization of, 139
men
    control of sexual act by, 106, 124
    decision to migrate made by, 5–6, 18, 20
    feminist attitudes toward, 61
    gay, 62, 132 n.1, 154
    loss of authority and status, 8, 24
    see also gender roles
menopause, 102–3
mental illness
    homosexuality and, 154–55
    from stress of migration, 22, 28, 31, 35, 150
migrant, term usage, 18
migration, term usage, 16
migration experience
    ambivalence from complexities of, 1–2, 30, 32, 34, 109, 113–14, 115, 119, 163
    bereavement compared to, 31–32
    commonalties shared across, 10, 13, 154, 162–66
    human developmental process compared to, 145
    identity and, see identity
    of immigrants vs. refugees, 16–18
    loss from, see loss
migration experience (cont.)
    psychological stages of, 20–23
    of single women, see single women
    stress resulting from, see stress
    from traditional vs. modern societies, 5
    women's social status impacting, 4

see also acculturation process; gender roles; language; narratives; sexuality

migration studies, women's experiences and, 2, 10, 18–19

Mishler, E. G., 54

morality
  gender role behaviors measuring family, 6, 45
  immigrant communities as guardians of, 6–7, 124–25, 128–32

mothers
  desire for sons, 97
  identity development of daughters and, 145–46, 163–64
  mental health of, 150
  migrating without children, 27, 73, 105
  patriarchal context of relations with daughters, 76–77, 151, 164
  percentage of refugees as, 3
  reactions to lesbian daughters, 66, 82–83, 116, 149
  sexual information supplied by, 68, 84, 87, 107, 146–48
  sexual information withheld by, 57, 64, 69, 79, 82, 91, 92, 99, 100, 106
  sexuality of, 62, 105, 147–48
  study of separation from daughters, 12–13, 49, 55, 112–18, 148–49
  see also daughters; families; gender roles; parents

mourning process, 16
  ambivalence toward migration experience and, 30, 32
  context of exit from home culture and, 29
  delayed, 31–32
  identifiable features of, 31
  see also grief; loss

Muñoz, M., 139

myths, *see* stereotypes

Narayan, Uma, 8, 130, 147

narratives
  Angela (Mexico), 69
  Annette (East Germany), 12, 112, 117–18, 148, 149, 151
  Aurelia (Australia/Thailand), 81–83, 89, 143
  Ayla (Turkey), 100–101
  Cecilia (Puerto Rico), 87–89, 149–50
  Cindy (Taiwan), 79–81, 89, 149, 158
  Colleen (Ireland), 12, 112, 115, 148, 151
  Cornelia (Perú), 108–9, 140
  Denise (Quebec), 101–3
  Eva (Austria), 84–86, 89, 149
  Hilde (Germany), 56, 61–63, 142, 144
  Inge (Germany), 69, 144
  Iris (Israel), 12, 118, 120–21
  Jazmin (Korea), 69–71, 142
  Judith (Russia), 110
  Kerrine (England/Jamaica), 72–75
  Leticia (Mexico), 67–68, 148
  Lin (Taiwan), 93–94, 130, 142
  Liv (Denmark), 110, 111–12
  Lorena (Puerto Rico), 76–79, 89, 139, 142, 156, 158
  Lucía (Perú), 106–8
  Manel (Sri Lanka), 98–99
  Marguerite (Austria), 56, 57–61, 142
  Marie-Claire (Haiti), 72–75
  Maritza (Cuba), 75–76, 88, 142, 149, 156, 158
  Maya (Netherlands), 86–87, 89, 144, 149, 156
  Mei (China), 91–93, 130, 142
  Mina (Iran), 12, 112, 114–15, 151
  Nora (Cuba), 12, 112, 116–17, 148
  Noriko (Japan), 94–97
  Novena (Russia), 12, 118, 119–20, 135

Olga (Cuba), 75, 76, 88, 156, 158
as research method, 37–42
Rivka (Europe), 110, 111, 130
Rosa (Nicaragua), 104–6
Roya (Iran), 12, 112, 113–14, 128, 148–49
Sandra (Mexico), 68
Shelo (Tibet/India), 89–91
Sissy (Korea), 97–98
Soledad (Brazil), 103–4
study of development and transformation of sexuality/gender roles, 11, 45, 48, 49, 55, 56
study of impacts of daughters' separation from mothers, 12–13, 49, 55, 112–18, 148–49
study of impacts of migration on adolescents, 11–12, 49, 50, 55, 118–21
Sudha (India), 69, 71–72
Sylvia (Jamaica), 72–75
text of interview questions guiding, 167–70
Ursula (Germany), 56, 64–67, 142, 144, 149
Violeta (Cuba), 12, 112, 116, 148, 149, 151
see also interview process
Necef, M. U., 5
Nicholson, P., 126–27
nude beaches, 65

Obejas, Achy, 34–35
obesity, 85, 86, 89
Ochberg, R. L., 39
Ogundipe-Leslie, 'Molara, 8
orgasm, 60
Padilla, A. M., 18
parents
adolescent rebellion against, 25, 36 n2, 75
adolescents separated from, 26–27, 32, 112–18, 148–49
first language different from children, 134–35
pace of children's acculturation and, 24, 119–20
protective roles of, 22, 24, 114, 115, 116, 135, 147
racism of, 99
reactions to daughters' lesbianism, 65–67, 82–83, 87, 88–89, 116, 149, 157, 158
rigidity of, resulting from immigration, 7, 80–81
see also daughters; families; fathers; mothers
Paris, J., 26
Parker, A., 124
Parkes, L. M., 31, 33
pathologies, *see* mental illness
patriarchy
control of sexuality and, 129
decision to migrate and, 5, 18, 20
impacts of migration on, 3, 125–26, 163
mother-daughter relationships and, 76–77, 151, 164
Pedraza, Sylvia, 19, 24
persecution
political, 16, 28–29, 36 n1
for sexual orientation, 75, 154, 155, 156
see also refugees
Phoenix, A., 159
place (geographical), importance of, 33–35
Plummer, K., 39, 41–42
political asylum, sexual orientation as grounds for, 155
political persecution, 16, 28–29, 36 n1
see also refugees
Polkinghorne, D. E., 38, 39, 40
pornography, 62
Portes, Alejandro, 16, 17, 18, 21, 136, 140
posttraumatic stress, 16, 17, 28

power
  language and, 134, 135
  loss of, through racism, 7, 70
  male-female relations and, 6, 18,
    19, 23, 69, 76–77, 92, 106
  narrative research methodology
    and, 41
  see also authority
Prieto, Yolanda, 130
promiscuity, 6
prostitution, forced, 36 n1
psychological effects of immigration
  across generations, 15–16, 86
  contexts of exit and reception expe-
    riences, 16, 21, 28–29
  depression, 28, 32, 107, 150
  grief, 16, 30, 31–33
  internalization of oppression, 8
  loss, see loss
  mental illness, 22, 150
  questioning what could have been,
    33–35, 111, 157–58
  stages of migration experience, 20–23
psychology discipline
  impacts of historical events omitted
    from, 15
  narratives as research method in,
    37–42
psychotherapy
  role of narrative in, 37–38
  significance of language in, 136–37,
    139, 141

racism
  difficulties of acculturation from,
    9–10, 22, 27–28, 71–75, 164
  lesbians and, 156, 158–59
  loss of power from, 7, 70
  of parents, 99
  stereotypes and, 8, 70, 71–72, 94,
    99, 108, 164
rape, 20, 90, 129, 132
  war and, 28, 36 n1, 124
rapprochement stage, separation from

parents impacting, 26
refugees
  difficulty of periodic return to
    homeland, 26–27, 28
  immigrants vs., 16–18
  percentage of women as, 3
  stress from experiences as, 16,
    17–18, 19, 20, 28–29, 35, 92
rejection
  of host culture as coping mecha-
    nism, 22, 120–21
  of lesbians in immigrant communi-
    ties, 153, 154, 157
  of marriage, 102
  sense of, by host culture, 19
relationships, see daughters; families;
  fathers; friendship networks; marriage; mothers; narratives; romantic
  relationships
religion
  acculturation process and, 22, 71,
    115
  influencing sexual behavior, 58, 64,
    76, 92–93, 100, 125, 126
relocation process, see migration experience
Reno, Janet, 155
Renzetti, C. M., 41
respect, 23, 92, 100
  lacking in U. S. for authority, 73,
    112
Rodríguez-Nogués, L., 32
Rogler, L. H., 5, 29, 34
role models, 77, 100, 146–48,
  164
  see also mothers; parents
romantic relationships
  interracial, 70, 80, 81, 99, 105–6,
    108
  intimacy and language in, 165–66
  intraracial, 71, 74, 75, 102–3
  see also marriage
Rosenwald, George C., 38–39, 47
Rubin, H. J., 44

Rubin, I. S., 44
Rumbaut, Ruben G., 16, 17, 18, 21, 136, 140
Russo, M., 124

sadness, 28, 30
  see also depression
safety, sense of, preserved through gender roles, 7
Salgado de Snyder, V. N., 18
Schneider, M., 157
Schreier, Barbara, 126, 128
self-esteem, 19, 97, 139–40
sexism, see male superiority
sex roles, see gender roles
sexual abuse
  in families, 87, 129
  see also rape
sexual harassment, 58
sexuality
  acculturation process and, 6–7, 74, 76, 78, 82, 125, 128–32, 164
  adolescent rebellion and, 25, 36 n2, 75
  clothing and, 125–28
  comfort/discomfort of interviewees when addressing, 45, 67, 138–39, 141–42
  cultural variability of, 123–25, 132 n.1, 156
  expectations of, in immigrant communities, 6, 8, 76, 78, 101, 124–25, 128–32
  fear of, 60, 131, 148
  language and, see language and sexuality
  as measure of morality, 6–7, 45, 124–25, 128–32
  religion influencing, 58, 64, 76, 92–93, 100, 125, 126
  study of development and transformation of, 11, 45, 48, 49, 55, 56
  see also gay men; heterosexuals; lesbians
sexual orientation, see gay men; heterosexuals; lesbians
silence
  communicating values through, 146, 147, 148, 149
  see also mothers, sexual information withheld by
single women
  acculturation process for, 25–27, 146, 149
  grief and, 31–32
  stress for mothers of, 151
  study on separation from mothers, 12–13, 49, 55, 112–18, 148–49
social networks, see friendship networks
sociolinguistic theory, 142–43
Sommer, D., 124
Spark, C. M., 33
stereotypes
  racial, 8, 70, 71–72, 94, 99, 108, 164
  sexual, 70, 71, 94, 99, 108, 128–29, 130, 164
Stewart, Abigail, 164, 165
Stonequist, E. V., 22
stories, see narratives
stress
  acculturation process and, 22
  from loss of daughters to migration, 151
  from loss of home culture, 29–33
  of refugees, 16, 17–18, 19, 20, 28–29, 35, 92
  see also psychological effects of immigration
substance abuse, 22, 112
success
  grief masked by, 16, 31–32
  social status of women and, 4
support networks, see friendship networks

Telles, P., 31
Todd, Emmanuel, 4

Torres, L., 141

torture, 28–29, 36 n1

tradition

oppression of immigrants through sensitivity to, 8–9

preservation of, through women's sexual behavior, 6–8, 13, 22–24, 123–25, 128–32, 149

see also gender roles; values

Tremble, B., 157

Trumbach, R., 124

United States

attitudes toward immigrants in, 16, 25, 120, 139–40

attitudes toward sex in, 61, 64–65, 69, 70–71, 87, 92–93, 101, 144

disrespect for authority in, 73, 112

foreign-born population in, 3

immigration policies, 73, 154–56

sexism in, 150

socioeconomic classes of immigrants to, 46–47

torture and abuse survivors in, 29

see also racism

values

communicating, through silence, 146, 147, 148, 149

language reflecting cultural, 143

migration experience destabilizing, 19, 21, 25, 32–33

see also gender roles; tradition

violence against women, *see* domestic violence; rape

virginity, importance of, in home cultures, 6, 59, 62, 68, 109, 130

vocabulary, *see* language

war

rape and, 28, 36 n1, 124

see also refugees

Weiss, R. S., 53

Wierzbicka, Anna, 136

Woollett, A., 126–27

Yaeger, P., 124

Yuval-Davis, Nira, 6, 125